# The Scrappy Entrepreneur

# The Scrappy Entrepreneur

## *How to Effectively Lead an Innovation-Driven Startup*

Véronique Peiffer

BEP

BUSINESS EXPERT PRESS

Leader in applied, concise business books

The Scrappy Entrepreneur:
How to *Effectively* Lead an Innovation-Driven Startup

Cover design by Véronique Peiffer

Interior design by S4Carlisle Publishing Services, Chennai, India

First published in 2025 by
Business Expert Press, LLC
222 East 46th Street, New York, NY 10017
www.businessexpertpress.com

ISBN-13: 978-1-63742-850-4 (paperback)
ISBN-13: 978-1-63742-851-1 (e-book)

Business Expert Press Entrepreneurship and Small Business Management Collection

First edition: 2025

10 9 8 7 6 5 4 3 2 1

**EU SAFETY REPRESENTATIVE**
Mare Nostrum Group B.V.
Mauritskade 21D
1091 GC Amsterdam
The Netherlands
gpsr@mare-nostrum.co.uk

# Description

**Innovation-driven entrepreneurship is hard. Let this book make it easier for you.** You have a business idea that you truly believe in. The extensive market research that you have done has made you even more *passionate about pursuing your idea*. Before you can start selling, you will need significant amounts of funding to develop your product and/or successfully meet mandatory regulatory requirements. You will also need help from people with skillsets that complement yours. If you find yourself in this situation, this book is for you.

Drawing on her *own first entrepreneurship experience* with medical technology startup palmm Co., author Véronique Peiffer, PhD, gets to the nuts and bolts of three key topics tailored to scrappy entrepreneurs—those who need to be extra resourceful to push their companies to the next phase:

- Fundraising,
- Hiring and managing a startup team,
- Dealing with the many less exciting but necessary aspects of creating and running a business, such as bookkeeping, document management, vendor selection, and more.

The book helps you know what to expect and even includes *simple spreadsheet templates* that can save you considerable time and money. The hard-won learnings from *seven other medtech entrepreneurs* provide additional perspectives. Ultimately, reading this book will make any first-time entrepreneur feel better-prepared for the real deal.

## Keywords/Phrases

First-time founder; Early-stage funding for startups; Finding startup investors; How to build startup team; How to start a business without money; Practical guide to starting a business; Entrepreneurship course

# Contents

# List of Figures and Tables

## Figures

## Tables

# Review Quotes

*"Seeing opportunities and challenges with fresh eyes is a big advantage for innovators. Véronique Peiffer's* The Scrappy Entrepreneur *has this kind of clear-eyed quality. Her description of the entrepreneurial process can only have come from someone who has just emerged from the trenches. The result is a fresh and practical guide that will appeal to both aspiring and experienced entrepreneurs."*—**Professor Emeritus Paul Yock, Founding Director, Stanford Biodesign**

*"The Scrappy Entrepreneur* is packed with resources, advice, and lessons that any early-stage entrepreneur can benefit from. Reading this book feels like being supported by a great mentor—answering countless questions that I had myself at the start of my entrepreneurial journey and that I now hear from so many others at the start of theirs. A perfect read for anyone looking to get off to the right start as a scrappy entrepreneur."*—**Amanda French, Innovator, entrepreneur, and adviser (Founding CEO—Emme, acquired)**

*"Véronique Peiffer shares her hard-earned lessons on big and small aspects of entrepreneurship. Her guidance is rooted in firsthand experience from her own startup, which I had the privilege of working with during its earliest days. Each chapter combines anecdotes, reflections, and practical advice, thoughtfully addressing the nuances of different startups. I'll recommend this book to all the early-stage founders I work with—it shows that they are not alone in navigating funding, team dynamics, and all the small stuff."*—**Christina Tamer, Vice President, Ventures at VentureWell**

*"A proven way to maximize a startup's chance of success is to learn from those who have done it before. This book should be one of the "coaches" early-stage entrepreneurs turn to for guidance in navigating the complexities of running a startup—efficiently, cost-effectively, and with confidence. Drawing on her own experience, Véronique Peiffer delves into the nuts and bolts of essential topics for any startup company, from fundraising and team building to time-consuming but unavoidable tasks like document management and insurance. This book is required reading for any entrepreneur for whom money and time are precious resources."*—**Andrew Cleeland, CEO, Fogarty Innovation**

# Introduction

No one who has done it will tell you that entrepreneurship is easy. In fact, the odds are against you: The vast majority of startups inevitably fail (Startup Genome LLC 2019). "It's like running a marathon in a minefield," says serial entrepreneur Kim Hvidkjaer in *How to F\*ck Up Your Startup* (Hvidkjaer 2022). Speaking from my own experience, there are certainly days that feel that way!

Time is money. In a young, underfunded company, this expression can be taken quite literally. You are constantly making trade-off decisions about where your time is best spent. Should you talk to another investor candidate or use that hour to make progress on the technology you're developing? Or maybe invest that time in looking for someone who can do the work for you?

To complicate things further, a gazillion distractions that are urgent but not mission-critical keep coming your way. Think registrations that need to be kept up to date and choices that need to be made about whether to buy software or outsource payroll, accounting, tax, program management, and so on. In the beginning, you won't mind spending some time on all of this, particularly if it can save the company money. But as all these tasks start to add up, you realize that time is ticking away and none of this is helping you get closer to reaching your company goal. If you have sufficient cash, you can outsource less thrilling tasks and hire people with specialized expertise so that you can focus on what you do best. However, for the scrappy entrepreneur—the one who never has more than a handful of employees and typically less than a year of runway left—that approach is not an option.

When I got curious about entrepreneurship, which wasn't until after completing a PhD in aeronautics/bioengineering and spending a couple of years in management consulting, I started reading about it. The textbook *Biodesign: The Process of Inventing Medical Technologies* (Zenios et al. 2009) catalyzed my decision: I have always been passionate about medicine, and that book helped me see how I, as an engineer with business experience, could contribute to the future of health care in major ways. Through real-life examples, it showed me that it is possible to identify a true, unmet clinical need, invent a viable solution, and commercialize it. Even though this is not an easy feat, it sounded like a challenge worth pursuing. The book introduced me to various elements involved in inventing medical devices, including securing intellectual property (IP) and appreciating the complexities of the regulatory and reimbursement processes that come with innovation in health care. But it did not detail the intricacies of founding and running a company.

Books such as *The Lean Startup* (Ries 2011), *The Startup Owner's Manual* (Blank and Dorf 2020), *The Hard Thing about Hard Things* (Horowitz 2014), *Venture Deals* (Mendelson and Feld 2019), and *Peak* (Conley 2007) helped me gain a high-level understanding of product–market fit, company strategy, fundraising, and hiring and managing a team. However, the solutions offered were often more applicable to startups that were bigger and better-funded than mine.

Sometimes an entrepreneur can get away with *bootstrapping*—building a business without taking on any external investment. *Strategic Bootstrapping* (Rutherford 2015) is a helpful read in that regard. For my startup and other *innovation-driven startups* (including the majority of life sciences companies), that is generally not an option, as significant amounts of money are needed for research and development (R&D) and to successfully meet mandatory regulatory requirements prior to commercialization.

Despite having done a bunch of reading, there were also many aspects of entrepreneurship that I ended up learning about only by living through the experience. It seems that topics that are less exciting than fundraising and team building just don't get airtime, even if every entrepreneur encounters them.

This is why I am putting pen to paper. I want to help early entrepreneurs spend more of their time doing what matters. I'm particularly focused on those launching innovation-driven startups who do not yet have the capital to solve problems by outsourcing or expanding the team. These are the ones who need to be extra resourceful for multiple years on end—the scrappy entrepreneurs.

To be clear, this will not be a step-by-step guide to all elements of starting and running a business, as I focus only on a subset of topics that were glaringly missing in other books and teaching materials. I want to help you find resources to kick-start you on tasks that are urgent but not necessarily important for your project, the things that end up costing you more time than the fun stuff you signed up for. I want to help you make quicker decisions, particularly when it comes to fundraising and building your team, as these are two critical aspects of running a startup venture. To do it, I will provide tools and resources I developed for my own use, including simple spreadsheet templates that have delighted other entrepreneurs when I have shared them in the past. Visit veroniquepeiffer.com to receive a copy of the Scrappy Entrepreneur's toolkit.

Along the way, you'll get to hear how I worked through all this with palmm, the company I cofounded in 2017 to stop excessive hand sweat. This not-often-talked-about condition, medically termed *palmar hyperhidrosis*, affects 2 percent of the general population (Doolittle et al. 2016) and makes everyday practices like shaking hands a mortifying experience. I set out to help those sufferers. You'll learn about our highs and lows and find out how we did over the course of this book.

As every venture has its own nuances, I've asked several fellow entrepreneurs who went through, or are still going through, the scrappy phase, to share and add their perspectives on specific topics. All in all, my goal is to make as many first-time entrepreneurs as possible feel better-prepared for the real deal.

Before we begin, there are a few important caveats:

- First, this book is not a substitute for doing your own research and networking. Even the best-prepared entrepreneur needs a network to fall back on for timely questions and advice, to leverage for fundraising, and to help with finding potential contributors, moral support, and so on.
- Second, this book does not offer legal advice. I have never talked to more attorneys than I did during my work at palmm and don't see a way around that for any entrepreneur. I highly recommend that you find reliable corporate and patent attorneys to help you on your journey.

- Third, the views and opinions expressed in this book are my own. They do not necessarily reflect the views or opinions of any of my past or current employers.
- Fourth, the vendors called out in this book are those that I have worked with or heard of. These callouts do not constitute or imply endorsement. There are likely other vendors on the market worth evaluating.
- And finally, my startup experience is in medical device technology. The entrepreneurs whose experiences are captured in the "From Another Perspective" inserts also work in this sector. Many aspects of this book can be relevant to any innovation-driven startup, but there will always be industry-specific nuances that I cannot capture because of my single industry perspective. For example, in the health care industry, it is typically the requirement for review by the Food and Drug Administration (FDA) prior to commercialization that drives the need for outside capital. In other industries, different drivers might be at play. Please be mindful of such nuances as you read this book and translate learnings to your industry.

With these caveats out of the way, let's dive in. The first section of this book focuses on fundraising for scrappy entrepreneurs who lead innovation-driven startups. The second section covers building a team on a limited budget, and the unexpected situations that may come your way in this regard. And the last section is dedicated to helping you navigate the many required, but noncritical, tasks that will inevitably demand your time and attention on your path to success.

# PART 1

# Fundraising

Fundraising as the first topic in a book about entrepreneurship may seem like the wrong place to begin. It's rarely the first thing you can accomplish when starting a company. Only a select few (likely serial, undoubtedly already successful) entrepreneurs get that privilege. You generally need to have at least a solid idea that closes a market gap and a well-thought-out business proposition before you can hit the fundraising road. Still, fundraising is the topic that many first-time entrepreneurs are hungriest to learn about. You may already have the solution concept in your mind and feel strongly that you'll be able to build out a full business plan using your existing knowledge, skills, and network. But you need to know if you'll be able to raise the dollars necessary to bring that idea to fruition and don't know how to get started on that front.

That was the situation I found myself in when my cofounder-to-be, Justin Huelman, and I were exploring the idea of treating excessive hand sweat. We had identified an unmet need, vetted it through patient interviews and surveys, and come up with a medical device solution that had potential. We'd been able to do all that, and more, with minimal help from others. But to develop, build, and test an actual product, we needed money. Based on benchmarking with comparable companies, we estimated we'd need well over $10 million if we followed a lean approach and up to $150 million if we were to take an aggressive path to market.

We had participated in a health technology innovation fellowship at Stanford University (called the Biodesign Innovation Fellowship) that had taught us how to innovate in health care and expanded our networks to include a good number of wealthy individuals and connections to angel groups and venture capital (VC) firms. But we did not really know the *best* way to tap into those networks without squashing opportunities and wasting time by engaging too quickly. Which investor candidates should we approach first and how much money should we ask them for?

Should we accept every offer to get introduced to potential investors? How should we gauge their interest in our opportunity, and what questions should we ask to determine whether they had money available to invest at all?

In this section of the book we'll get into who to ask for money (Chapter 1) and what to prepare (Chapter 2).

# CHAPTER 1

# Who to Ask for Money

Early-stage funding for innovation-driven startups can come from the following funding types: (1) pitch competitions, (2) grants, (3) incubators/accelerators, (4) individual angel investors, (5) angel groups, (6) collaborators and customers, (7) VC, and (8) strategic companies. Each funding type comes with its own advantages and drawbacks. We'll discuss those in more detail and assess when is the earliest optimal time to seek out these potential sources of money.

## 1. A Practical Example

Once we had early data indicating that our solution concept could work, Justin and I started applying for pitch competitions and grants, talking with angels, getting introduced at angel groups, and presenting to VCs—all at the same time! Ultimately, we applied to nine business pitch competitions, eight grants, and seven incubators/accelerators before even having incorporated a company. We spent less time approaching the other types of potential funders in that early phase but did our best to get a sense of their interest through pitches to a handful of individual angels, two angel groups, three VCs, and even a large, established company in our industry (also referred to as a *strategic*).

We ended up living for the first 2 years off pitch competition winnings and grant funding. This was possible thanks to some level of success—we received between $1,000 and $100,000 from seven out of nine pitch competitions and four out of eight grant applications—a very decent success rate if you ask me! Those funds allowed us to build initial prototypes and run a clinical *proof-of-concept* study. In this type of study, a small number of patients (about a dozen in our case) get to use a rudimentary version of the envisioned technology to find out if there is any signal indicating it may actually work. Ours demonstrated that we could significantly reduce the amount of hand sweat using a wearable treatment device—something that had never been done before. While the data were very promising, we also observed a few critical ease-of-use constraints that we'd want to engineer around. All of this early work remained in the university setting, and we were eligible for some of the grants thanks to that academic affiliation.

Even though the clinical data were based on a product concept that would need to be modified extensively, it convinced the staff at one incubator, called Fogarty Institute for Innovation (now Fogarty Innovation), that we had the grit needed to get a company off the ground. Based on our pitch and their own background research, they also agreed with us that the unmet need we were looking to address was a real one. They invested $100,000 and accepted us into their program[1]—a validation that ultimately made it easier for us to get angel investors excited to participate in our seed investment round. This is when we incorporated a business, as we needed an entity to accept the incubator's money.

After multiple tries, we also had luck with another accelerator, the Stanford-affiliated StartX program. StartX brought us together with other founders in biweekly meetups over a period of 3 months and provided mentoring support, access to a new network of entrepreneurs, and participation in pitch events. StartX also provided an option to rent office space at a reduced cost, but we passed on that since we had office space through Fogarty Innovation.

So, here we were, a year and a half after the initial light bulb had gone off, having spent a good bunch of the initial pitch competition and grant funding (about $275,000) but now refueled with money and support from both a well-respected incubator and an accelerator program. We knew that we had extensive R&D work ahead of us, as well as the typical regulatory steps required for a medical device before we would be allowed to commercialize any product. This would cost us at least an order of magnitude more than what we had in the bank. We knew that pitch competitions and grants alone would not be able to get us there, so we had to start securing other types of funding.

Other companies-in-residence at Fogarty Innovation that were a few years ahead of us had been able to make progress through a combination of grant funding, angel investments, and angel groups. After considering those three sources, we decided to focus our efforts at this stage on (individual) angel investors. In the spirit of *go big or go home*, several mentors had recommended that we no longer spend time applying for grants. The applications take a significant amount of time to write and perfect, months pass before you hear back, it takes more time reapplying if you're unsuccessful, and awards can be narrow in terms of allowed use of funds. We listened to that advice, but I'll tell you more about this decision later (see the "From Another Perspective" insert on page 12).

With regard to angel groups, feedback from other entrepreneurs was mixed. While some were happy with the investments they had received from such groups, others confided that they had spent a lot of time getting in with angel groups without any resulting investment. A few entrepreneurs also told us that they had experienced issues with the requirements that had come with the angel group investment, particularly as it related to board seats. (In each case, the angel group insisted that one of their members sit on the company's board of directors to have more of a say in the company's decision-making, but later-stage investors wanted to reverse that decision.) Based on this input, Justin and I made the decision to hold off from aggressively pursuing angel group funding at that time.

The individual angel investor connections offered to us by fellow incubator companies became key starting points. We were also able to participate in a virtual pitch event organized by StartX, which gave us new connections to potential investors. In addition, we tapped into our personal networks to get more introductions to wealthy individuals and ask them to invest in our company. Overall, we were able to secure $475,000 in angel investments for our *convertible note* seed round.[2]

Something that was not clear to me before raising this seed round is that the money raised in a *round* does not all have to hit the company's bank account at the same time. Generally, there is a window in which the documents state the money needs to come in, but it is possible to push back these dates—as long as all stakeholders sign an agreement that includes this provision. Between the first and last dollars received for our seed round, almost a year and a half had lapsed. As a result, we had already spent quite a bit of the total by the time the last dollars arrived, and we needed to start looking for more funds right away again.

At this stage, I had a really hard time deciding what the right amount of money to ask for would be, as we could take a variety of different approaches. On the one hand, we could build a minimal viable product and aim to get the green light from the FDA for commercialization as quickly as possible, thereby de-risking the regulatory process. This approach would require a raise of $2 million. Alternatively, we could invest a lot more in product development and clinical testing upfront to help us get buy-in from the physician community prior to commercialization. That approach would require closer to $15 million.

Someone suggested we prepare two pitch decks in parallel: one for a larger amount to put in front of VCs, and one for a smaller amount to put in front of individual angels and angel groups. It takes considerably more work to prepare two different versions of your story, and it may be harder to keep track at times, but it is not wrong. There really are multiple ways of taking an idea to market. As long as you don't have an investment round open yet, you can let the two options play out against each other.

For reasons I'll explain later, we were not successful at closing this next investment round. However, I do feel strongly that the two-story approach was the right one, and I would absolutely consider that strategy again for any future venture.

## 2. Overview of Funding Types

Now that you have an idea of where one startup got its early money from, let's discuss each funding type separately. I'd like to give you a sense of advantages and drawbacks for each and, consequently, when is the best time to apply for or engage with each of them. Where I can, I'll include resources to help you find investor candidates, as that's certainly one of the tricky aspects of fundraising. Table 1.1 provides a summary for your reference.

## 3. Pitch Competitions

There are many organizations that award prizes for *the best* startups.

### Pros and Cons

Pitch competitions are generally free for participants, other than costs incurred traveling to meeting venues. The key thing to consider is that participating in these public events forces you out of stealth mode. You

Table 1.1 *Overview of funding types with pros and cons, info on when to engage/apply, and typical check size*

| Funding type | Pros | Cons | Recommended minimum must-haves before you engage/apply | Typical time to engage/apply | Typical check size[a] |
|---|---|---|---|---|---|
| *Pitch competitions* | • No/low monetary cost<br>• Nondilutive<br>• May help get you connected to other potential investors | • Not possible to remain in full stealth mode | • Best assessed based on companies that have been successful in the past | • Best assessed based on companies that have been successful in the past | $1K–50K |
| *Grants* | • No/low monetary cost<br>• Nondilutive<br>• May help get you connected to advocates in your industry | • Significant time investment (preparing application, wait times, budget tracking)<br>• Can be narrow in terms of use of funds | • Typically clearly described in the application instructions | • As long as you consider your company to be underfunded (certainly for grants with >$50K check size) | $10K–2M |
| *Incubators/ accelerators* | • Various types of support offered, depending on the particular incubator/ accelerator<br>• Expands your network of fellow entrepreneurs<br>• Some come with a prestigious name brand | • Hard to gauge value upfront<br>• May be harder to remain in stealth mode<br>• Costs very much dependent on the particular incubator/ accelerator model | • Clear idea to solve an unmet need | • Typically earlier is better (e.g., prior to or at the time of incorporation) | $0–500K |

(continued)

Table 1.1 Overview of funding types with pros and cons, info on when to engage/apply, and typical check size (continued)

| Funding type | Pros | Cons | Recommended minimum must-haves before you engage/apply | Typical time to engage/apply | Typical check size[a] |
|---|---|---|---|---|---|
| *Individual angel investors* | • Relatively low burden of proof | • Time investment and luck needed to get connected to the right wealthy individuals for your opportunity<br>• Cap table[b] expands if you take on a lot of small checks<br>• Dilutive | • Clear idea to solve an unmet need<br>• Strong founding team | • Once you have minimum must-haves and until the round gets too big (e.g., >$3M) | $10K–250K |
| *Angel groups* | • Opportunity to get exposure to larger number of wealthy individuals in one go<br>• Some come with a prestigious name brand | • Dilutive<br>• Potentially other requirements in the deal (e.g., board seat)<br>• Sometimes presentation fees<br>• Need to manage angel group dynamics to be successful | • Clear idea to solve an unmet need<br>• Strong (founding) team<br>• Insider support<br>• Momentum for progress (without this funding) over the next 6 months | • Once you have minimum must-haves and until the round gets too big (e.g., >$10M) | $10K–2M |
| *Collaborators and customers* | • Various, depending on the type of investment<br>• Can be milestone-based so that you don't lose cash or stock if milestones are not reached | • Not as flexible as having cash in terms of spending options<br>• Need level of certainty that collaborator will remain relevant over time<br>• Need clear contract | • Clear idea to solve an unmet need<br>• For vendors, clear (tech) plan and how the vendor may fit into it | • Once you have a well-thought-through business proposition and until the round gets too big (e.g., >$3M) | $1K–$XM |

| | | | | | |
|---|---|---|---|---|---|
| *Venture capital* | • Typically larger investment potential, with ability to up investments in future rounds<br>• Typically transparent about their investment focus and potential | • Dilutive<br>• Likely other asks in the deal (e.g., board seat, preferred stock) | • Clear idea to solve an unmet need<br>• Strong team in place and/or strong proof of concept<br>• Established relationship with the VC | • Depending on the scope of the VC<br>• Once you have minimum must-haves | $500K–$XM |
| *Strategic companies* | • Larger investment potential<br>• Validation of the opportunity<br>• Builds relationship with potential acquirer | • Dilutive<br>• Potentially other asks in the deal (e.g., right of first refusal, requirement to align processes)<br>• May deter other companies from wanting to acquire you | • Clear idea to solve an unmet need<br>• Strong proof of concept<br>• Strong team for execution | • Depending on the scope of incubator/venture arm if available<br>• Once you have minimum must-haves | $500K–$XM |

[a]Typical check size is based on knowledge of the medtech industry in the late 2010s and early 2020s.
[b]A cap table or capitalization table is a document that lists the company's owners and ownership stake.

don't know who will be reading your application, and, if you're invited to present on stage, you will have to divulge at least some details about what you're doing to make your story compelling.

## When to Apply

To determine the optimal time to participate in pitch competitions, I recommend reviewing companies that have been prize winners in the past. Evaluate what milestones related to R&D, IP, and commercialization they had achieved when they participated, and how long they had been around. Some startups are based on concepts that have been in the making for multiple years and have lots of supporting research behind them. With palmm, we applied to MedTech Innovator—a nonprofit global pitch competition and accelerator for medical device, digital health, and diagnostic companies—about a year and a half after zeroing in on the unmet need of excessive hand sweat. Other participating companies had been in existence for more than 5 years. For this example, I wouldn't say that we would have benefited from waiting longer to apply. In fact, the $10,000 we won through the video competition component was timely for us. However, we should at least have considered increasing our chances to win the bigger $500,000 prize money by waiting a year or two.

When you're assessing the age of a competing company, note that the founding year is not always indicative of the age of the idea. The idea may have been developed in an academic setting and licensed at a later date, as was the case for palmm. Information on patents may give you further insight into these types of situations. Search the United States Patent and Trademark Office (USPTO)'s Patent Center (https://patentcenter.uspto.gov) and other databanks such as Google Patents (https://patents.google.com) to find these details. You can review the LinkedIn page of the company, its founders, and its employees to gain additional insight into the history of the company's idea.

## Resources to Find Pitch Competitions

When it comes to finding pitch competitions that may be the right fit for your startup, it generally requires both searching and asking around.

The list in our Scrappy Entrepreneur's toolkit can help get you started (see page 53 for details on how to access this toolkit). Pitch competitions come and go, so make sure you do your own research to ascertain which ones no longer exist, have changed in scope, or are entirely new.

# 4. Grants

There are many different types of grants, but, in general, grants are funds provided by an organization with an interest in advancing R&D and commercialization in a particular area. Grants are often awarded based solely on written applications.

### Pros and Cons

Like pitch competitions, grants typically come at no monetary cost and are nondilutive (meaning that you do not have to give up any equity in exchange for receiving the funds—a major advantage). If the grant you're awarded comes from an organization that is known in your space, it may even help connect you with relevant advocates for your technology.

On the flipside, grants often require a significant time investment both to prepare the application and to track spending according to the budget requirements laid out for the particular grant. You need to specify upfront what percentage of the grant will be spent on specific tasks, and certain aspects of the work may not be covered by the grant. Additionally, funding cycles can be long. For example, for Small Business Innovation Research (SBIR) grants, you have to wait for about 6 months before you hear back, and another 6 months or so before you can start deploying the funds.

### When to Apply

Given the cons listed above, many believe that grants are only a good option prior to incorporation or for companies in their first months of existence. As I explained previously, this is why we stopped actively pursuing grants for palmm. This is indeed the right approach in times when venture capitalists are willing to invest early. However, in times when early venture money is very tight, grants can be a huge help to keep you afloat just when you need it. You'll hear more on this in the "From Another Perspective" insert below. If you don't have a solid investor base yet, I recommend you always keep an eye out for relevant grant opportunities and aim to have one or two applications in the pipeline at any given time.

### Resources to Find Grant Opportunities

In the United States, the government's SBIR and Small Business Technology Transfer (STTR) grant funding opportunities are well known. But there are other grants available as well, both from the government and from different organizations. These are often lesser known and are sometimes less competitive as a result. For example, with palmm we applied not only for SBIR grants from the National Institute for Health (NIH) and National Science Foundation (NSF) but also for non-SBIR grants from NIH such as the Director's Innovator Award and Pioneer Award because we were eligible based on my PhD and postdoc background. The FDA also had grant opportunities for medical device innovations with a pediatric component, which applied to us. Our university affiliations made us eligible for still other grants. And because we were working in the space of dermatology, we searched hard for grants from the American Association of Dermatology, other skin-focused institutes, and patient advocacy groups. Finally, we also looked for grants related to the mode of action of our technology—electrical stimulation. I'm sharing these examples to demonstrate that you need to think about all dimensions of your team, including location, industry, and product, when generating a grant target list.

## From Another Perspective: Grants to Help You Hit Milestones

As I mentioned earlier in this chapter, with palmm, we took a pause from applying for grants. In hindsight, I don't think that was the right decision, especially since we were in a time when venture capitalists weren't eager to invest early. The reason I would do it differently in the future is that I've seen many other scrappy entrepreneurs successfully leverage grants to put millions of dollars to work and achieve major milestones as a result. Holly Rockweiler, chief executive officer (CEO) and cofounder of women's health company Madorra, raised roughly $7 million in grant funding, including three large SBIR grants. Her company successfully completed two comprehensive (randomized control) clinical trials made possible by these grants. Holly shared her perspective on obtaining and maintaining grant funding with me:

> Grants are amazing sources of funding in many ways: They are nondilutive, can be substantial in size (over $2 million for certain SBIR grants), help boost your brand, and may come with other perks such as invitations to investor–entrepreneur meet-up conferences. While grant writing can be painful, I have often been able to put snippets from those written documents to use elsewhere. And the reference letters that we were required to collect turned out to be useful as well, as various stakeholders viewed those as meaningful endorsements from investors and potential acquirers.

Holly continued,

> Unfortunately, however, grants alone are not enough to keep a company going. There are restrictions on what they can fund, delays in when you get the money, and other stipulations that can make them cumbersome to work with. For example, to obtain one particular grant, we had to ask another entity to invest using a different financing structure (a Safe instead of a convertible debt note[2]), as the grant specifically restricted debt financing for its recipients. It was a complex situation for us that we wouldn't have been able to navigate without a good attorney on our side.

Holly's top tip for successful grant applications is to

> remember that there will be a human on the other side reading your document, someone who is probably doing this after

their daytime job. Make the text easy to follow, with sufficient context, images, and spacing between sections. We wrote one grant application ourselves but leveraged a grant writer for our next two SBIRs (thanks in part to a grant from the state of Oregon that provided funding to specifically support grant applications!). Getting the help from a grant writer was beneficial: Grant reviewers are often looking for specific elements in the application, and good grant writers know what those things are. For example, some grants are intended to help address complex technical questions that have potential applications beyond the one you are looking to immediately address. If such opportunities jump off the page in your application, you have an edge over your competition.

A final word of advice from Holly when it comes to managing grants: "Managing grant budgets takes time as well. Flag the expenses related to a grant in your accounting software. There is always a chance that you get audited, so it's important to get it right."

## 5. Incubators/Accelerators

The types of support incubators and accelerators offer to startups can include:

- Office space (including lab and manufacturing space)
- Cash investment
- Guidance and hands-on support from experienced mentors, entrepreneurs-in-residence, and engineers-in-residence
- Access to the leadership team's network of experts across the industry
- Access to tools and equipment for common use
- Sponsored interns
- Education on topics related to the startup world or relevant industry
- Invitations to pitch events to help attract investment.

I'm bucketing incubators and accelerators together as they are part of the same spectrum, although the support offered by incubators tends to be longer in duration than the support offered by accelerators. Each incubator or accelerator puts its own twist on the definition, so ensure you understand what you'll get.

### Pros and Cons

In addition to the support offered by the incubator/accelerator directly, startups can benefit from the community of other entrepreneurs that are part of the incubator/accelerator, something I found tremendously valuable. In fact, fellow entrepreneurs are often the ones with the most up-to-date, actionable advice. Joining a well-known incubator/accelerator has the additional intangible advantage of name/brand recognition.

The cost of joining an incubator or accelerator can vary widely. Some take an equity stake in the company, and there may be a (low) monthly rent, (discounted) hourly rates for tapping into entrepreneurs-in-residence, and more. The incubator/accelerator may also request your involvement to help showcase their work, which takes time and may preclude you from operating in stealth mode.

My recommendation is to only apply for an incubator/accelerator if their scope is entirely aligned with the objectives of your startup in terms of sector, company stage, mentor expertise, and so on. Otherwise, the services will probably not be as valuable as hoped. Also consider whether you already have capabilities in-house or easy/affordable access to these, as there is no need to duplicate support you already have. While I found tremendous value in being part of an incubator, a friend and founder of a women's health company decided not to join one. He was a more experienced, serial entrepreneur, and he had already set up his own tool shop in his garage, so he didn't think the cost–benefit trade-off was going to be favorable.

### When to Apply

Joining an incubator or accelerator is generally most beneficial early on when you have a small team and can truly leverage the mentorship and other support offered.

We participated in the StartX accelerator program when we had only just moved into Fogarty Innovation, the incubator in which we ended up residing for 4 years. In hindsight, we would have benefited from StartX more had the core networking sessions not taken place while we were getting settled at our incubator. For those couple of months, our time to invest in these new contacts became too thinly stretched, leaving us unable to fully leverage the resources we were offered.

There are also financial considerations that may influence optimal timing to join an incubator/accelerator. If the incubator/accelerator takes a fixed equity stake in your company, the relative cost of this is lower when it is taken earlier rather than later. As a hypothetical example, if an incubator gives $100,000 in return for a 6 percent stake of your company this means that they value your company at $1.67 million—regardless of how much work has already gone into it. Whether or not anti-dilution clauses are included in the contract matters as well here and is definitely worth discussing with an attorney.

### Resources to Find Incubator/Accelerators

Like identifying relevant pitch competition and grant opportunities, finding the right incubator/accelerator for your startup takes work.

Some programs, including Y Combinator and StartX, run across industries. You can also look for industry-specific incubators/accelerators such as the incubator we resided in with palmm. Incubators/accelerators can be independent organizations (such as Y Combinator, Fogarty Innovation, and Plug and Play Tech Center), or they can be linked to an academic institution (such as StartX and VentureStudio), to a strategic company (such as Gore's Gore Innovation Labs and Johnson & Johnson's JLabs), or to a venture fund (such as IndieBio). To find the right one for your startup, use the Internet and ask other founders for their opinions.

## 6. Individual Angel Investors

An angel investor is a funny term to describe an individual who gives money to a startup in exchange for ownership equity (or a note that can convert to ownership equity[3]). While there are technically no prerequisites for being an angel investor, it is easier for startups to limit themselves to taking money from angel investors who are *accredited*. As per the definition of the U.S. Securities and Exchange Commission (SEC) that is current in 2024, an accredited investor is simply:

1. "An individual with a net worth over $1 million, excluding primary residence (individually or with spouse or partner), or
2. An individual with gross income exceeding $200,000 in each of the 2 most recent years or joint income with a spouse or partner exceeding $300,000 for those years and a reasonable expectation of the same income level in the current year."

With the help of a lawyer, you can let an investor self-certify that they fulfill at least one of the accredited investor requirements. No other documents are needed.

If you decide to take on investors that are not sufficiently wealthy to be accredited, you'll have more paperwork to take care of (Nth round, n.d.).

### Pros and Cons

It takes a lot of time to find angel investors with a genuine interest in your idea, belief in your approach and team, and funds ready to commit to a high-risk venture. But on those occasions when I found such an individual, I noticed that I didn't need to show them that much to win them over. Over half of my angel investors made their investment decision after two or three meetings, during which I presented a total of maybe 20 slides and followed up occasionally with a journal article or more details on our market research. I am not insinuating that angel investors are less sophisticated. On the contrary, half of palmm's seed round angel investors were industry professionals who themselves have been successful in the startup world, 20 percent were physicians with specialties relevant to our space, and 10 percent were potential users of our technology. At the earliest stages of an innovation-driven venture, there just are still a lot of unknowns, and angel investors are willing to take on that risk with you. They'll spend less time evaluating each individual opportunity, realizing that they need a positive return on only a subset of their investments.

### When to Engage

The best way to know when you're ready to approach individual angel investors is by understanding when other entrepreneurs in your field started to get their first angel money in. Based on my experience, angel investors are typically looking for an unmet need they believe in and a founding team they can trust. With palmm, we experienced a great boost in our success with angel investor conversations after joining Fogarty Innovation, as that affiliation helped convince them that the founding team was strong and committed. You can always test the water by talking to a handful of angels to gauge your readiness, but realize that this will be time-consuming if you still need to find these investor candidates first.

### Resources to Find Individual Angel Investors

The best advice I can give you with regard to finding angel investors is this: Network! Tell people what you're doing, and show how excited you are about it. Seek out conferences and meetings where you might find interested individuals, get to know other entrepreneurs who may have relevant contacts for you in their network, and so on.

To give you a sense of how things may unfold, let me share with you how this worked out for us at palmm in the initial months of angel investor fundraising. After talking with many, many people in my network during those initial months, I logged a total of 30 angel investor candidates. Of those, five ended up investing in palmm. When I reflected on these numbers, I was positively surprised by this ultimate success rate of one in six. It seemed a lot lower when I was going through the process. But keep in mind that, to find these 30 wealthy individuals, I interacted with many more *connectors* in between.

People who decide not to invest sometimes offer to connect you with someone they know. Through the process I learned that it is generally not helpful to get introduced through someone who could be, but is not, an investor in your company. The recipient of such an introduction often wants to know if the connector is an investor. A negative response invariably causes the person receiving the introduction to be doubtful: Why did the connector not make an investment themselves (whether it's as an angel investor, as part of an angel group, or with their VC fund)? Even if there is a very logical explanation that has nothing to do with the business potential of your company, the new potential investor may, consciously or subconsciously, wonder if there is something else going on. The only exception is if the scope of investments of the connector is entirely different (e.g., you are a health care startup, but they are a fintech investor). Then, you may be able to get away with an intro like this. Even introductions from mentors who fall in this category can hurt you in this way. In those instances, it is better to ask for the name of the person they'd like to connect you with and then find a more neutral connector.

Fellow entrepreneurs are generally helpful connectors, particularly if they received an investment from the person they can introduce you to. At palmm, over a third of our individual angel investors came to us through fellow entrepreneur connectors, almost a quarter from incubator/accelerator-related events, another quarter from our own (pre-company) networks, 10 percent through our investors, and 10 percent through a mentor who is not an angel investor. Finally, keep in mind that it is important that the connector is a trusted individual. If they're not, it is better to avoid leveraging that person's network.

One more thought on how to find angel investors: Over the years, I perfected my technique of accepting introductions. A warm hand-off is key. This includes asking the connector to send an introductory email connecting you both, proposing to prepare the content of that introductory e-mail yourself to ensure it is crisp and enticing, and being the first to respond-all to that initial connection email with a short but excited ask for a conversation. Don't be disappointed if you have to send a reminder after a week. People get busy! Your timely reminders show that you're committed and on top of things. That said, don't go overboard either: If someone hasn't responded after three or four reminders spaced out by a week or two each, they likely don't want to engage. Park the name in your backlog (see page 47) and look opportunistically for an organic reconnection point.

## A Note on Investments from Family and Friends

When I started out as an entrepreneur, various mentors recommended that we do not take investment dollars from family and close friends but, instead, focus on people who had an angel investment portfolio or were looking to build one out. I am so happy that we followed that advice. You'll find out the reason for this closer to the end of this book as you learn more about palmm.

However, if you have family or close friends who happen to be the people who will add credibility to your venture, that is a different story. Their involvement could be even more beneficial if they're willing to make their name known to other potential investors and help advocate for your story. If you have such family or close friends and they are not ready to invest, you'd better tighten up your explanation and ensure it is aligned with theirs in case they are ever asked that question.

# 7. Angel Groups

An angel group is a group of wealthy individuals who meet at a regular cadence—for example, every other week or monthly—to hear selected startups pitch. When I first heard the term *angel group*, I assumed that these groups make their investment decisions together. That model does indeed exist: In those instances, the angel group has established a fund by collecting contributions from its members, and the decision to invest is made by some type of voting process. However, more often than not, angel group members make their investment decisions independently. The meetings are held as a way to meet entrepreneurs and hear their presentations, but if a member of such a group wants to invest, they do so of their own accord. In some angel groups, there is a third model, in which investment decisions are made individually, but if a sufficient number of members decide to participate, a special entity is created so that these members invest together in the company. The advantage of forming this entity is that only one line needs to be added to the company's cap table[4] as opposed to a bunch of individual names, resulting in less hassle when you need to get signatures from all stakeholders. Setting up such an entity does, however, add to attorney fees and may take more time.

The full process from the initial contact to dollars in the bank varies from one angel group to another and typically takes about 6 ($\pm$ 3) months. Some angel groups describe their process on their website. It usually starts with a written application, but it's worth preceding this with at least one informal meeting with a group member to understand what they are looking for. If you are selected based on your application, you get to present in front of the bigger group. Some angel groups have a *pay-to-play* model where they ask a fee for a place to present, even though the Angel Capital Association (ACA) advocates against this practice (Angel Capital Association 2024). After your presentation, the group decides whether there is sufficient interest to assess the company in more detail (referred to as *performing due diligence*).

### Pros and Cons

A key advantage of approaching angel groups is that you get exposure to a larger number of wealthy individuals in one go. However, I have personally found interacting with angel groups to be one of the most polarizing experiences of early fundraising. There are so many different factors that play a role and, as a result, angel group fundraising is even more of an art than with other funding types—one that I feel I never truly mastered, despite having engaged with more than 20 angel groups and gone into the diligence process with 3 of them.

To begin with, each group is a collection of individuals each of whom has their own opinion. These individuals can influence each other in unpredictable ways. You may have the impression that your presentation was very well received, only to hear afterwards that one individual strongly advocated against you during the debrief conversation, thereby squashing interest from others. Another quirk of angels who belong to angel groups is that they like to offer advice. I vividly remember a conversation with an angel group member during a due diligence meeting in which this individual told me that a different go-to-market approach would be better than the one I had detailed in my pitch. I had spent months thinking about this exact question, so I responded by explaining how I had come to my viewpoint. After the group had completed their diligence process and decided not to move forward with an investment, I heard through an insider that that particular person had gotten the impression that I was not open to feedback. My conviction had clearly come across as arrogance. Because I did not seem receptive to that one person, the opportunity had passed.

You may think that angel group members who participate in the meetings do so because they have capital available to spend on high-risk investments. Through interactions with group members, I learned that that is not always the case. Some angel group members were actively looking to invest when they joined the group years ago but now are waiting for their open investments to play out and enjoying more the company of their fellow members during these meetings than anything else. Others are there because they are entrepreneurs themselves, and they are looking to pitch to their friends soon. Still others attend because they want to get to know potential new clients for their business (e.g., they have a company that does R&D work, IP, legal, etc.). While such individuals may still invest, they may have different drivers behind their decisions. You can learn about these dynamics by talking with fellow entrepreneurs who have interacted with these angel groups. Just keep in mind that things change over time: Someone who was actively investing a year or two ago may not be an active investor today.

Angel groups invest to gain an equity stake in your company. They may have additional asks with their investment, such as getting a seat on the board of directors to have more of a say in the future of the company or becoming a board observer to gain additional insight and understanding of the company's progress.

I remember having an introductory conversation with a prominent member of an angel group, who started the meeting with questions about our deal terms before we even got to know each other or discussed the unmet need palmm was addressing. Luckily, this was the exception to the rule.

Finally, established angel groups often want the startup team to de-risk multiple key aspects before they feel comfortable jumping on the investment bandwagon.

Be aware that some of these groups are references for other groups. Getting an investment from such a group can help bring along other investors. But if you don't get in with that one, you risk having to explain why not. I recommend not officially pitching to such a reference group until you have a very good sense that they will invest, as a negative outcome may hurt you. If you have not gotten investment from a reference group but haven't presented to them yet, you can tell those who ask that you are still working on getting to know the right individuals there.

### When to Engage

While I was never able to successfully raise funds from an angel group for palmm, I have seen the most success when an entrepreneur is able to do the following two things:

- Gain *insider support* from a well-respected member of the group prior to the official presentation.
- Show momentum over the 6 months following the presentation, demonstrating the company is set up to succeed.

Both these elements contribute to angel group members getting FOMO—Fear of Missing Out—if they do not invest. And that will help win them over.

Let me explain both points more:

- Gaining *insider support*: If one group member is truly committed to investing prior to the official presentation, this person will help make a more convincing case to their fellow angels. A well-respected member will be able to rally the troops and get others to co-invest. Do not let this individual invest before you present to the group, as this may have the opposite effect. When that happens, the other group members may now think that the individual is trying to save their own past investment. If they have already invested in your company, consider asking them if they are willing to match new investments from group members up to a certain amount (e.g., up to $50,000) to demonstrate that they continue to be bold about the company's prospects.
- Demonstrating momentum post-presentation: Seeing traction is an important signal for every investor, but with angel groups it's even more important to get the timing right. Essentially, if you present to an angel group and they decide to kick off the diligence process, you have their attention. If, during the following months, you can de-risk a few aspects that they considered critical, you can increase their confidence in your ability to be successful. As a scrappy entrepreneur, this is particularly hard as you don't have a lot of resources in general, so you're probably

not looking for additional requirements as to what you should focus on. If you can get a sense of what high-risk elements they are most concerned about in advance (maybe through the insider who is already keen to invest), you can time your messaging about these elements better. Another great way to show momentum to angel groups is to announce a *lead investor* within this timeframe. A lead investor is typically the first investor who puts forward a sizeable chunk of funding and determines the deal terms. Especially if that lead investor is a well-known entity within your industry, this will help angel groups appreciate that you have a hot deal.

### Resources to Find Angel Groups

So, where do you find these angel groups? There are dozens of angel groups out there, often with a specific industry focus, or subgroups with a certain area of focus. The ACA lists a whole lot on their website (https://angel capitalassociation.org/directory/), but there are plenty more that aren't listed. Make sure to ask fellow entrepreneurs who they have come across.

New types of angel groups have emerged over the years. For example, palmm was featured on an angel investing platform, a website where angels can browse company profiles to find ones they'd like to invest in. The platform owners generally take a percentage of every investment to cover their costs. Once your profile is online, you can post updates to demonstrate traction. This will help increase traffic and visibility for your company. Keep in mind that doing this well takes time and resources. And sometimes, these platforms themselves come and go, as is the case for the one palmm was featured on.

## 8. Collaborators and Customers

When looking for funding, why not involve those with whom you'll be exchanging money anyways? I'm thinking of team members, collaborators more broadly, and even customers.

Strategic companies could also be included here, but we'll cover those separately in the *Strategic Companies* section on page 28.

### Pros and Cons

In a way, having a team member work partly for equity instead of for cash is a form of funding. It's a logical choice for most startups. The only complexity lies in determining appropriate terms, which we'll come back to in the *Hiring* section on page 73.

Some third-party vendors are willing to set up flexible payment terms, which can include compensation in the form of company stock. You can include milestone requirements in the contract so that you don't lose cash or stock if things don't work out. With palmm, we strongly considered this approach with a few R&D and design firms.

I don't recommend proactively seeking this type of funding. It's just something to consider once you have found a vendor you like and if you don't have the right resources to get them going. You'll want to have some level of certainty that this vendor will remain relevant to your company over a decent amount of time (I would argue a year at the minimum) to avoid adding to so-called *dead equity*.[5]

This type of funding cannot be your only funding source: It can be a way to get a certain type of work done, but really nothing else.

You may have heard of websites such as Kickstarter and Indiegogo. On these websites, individuals can buy product prior to the actual release date, which can help take the company over the finish line of manufacturing and delivering product. For innovation-driven companies like palmm, this is likely not a good option given that clearing regulatory hurdles takes too much time and money for a typical crowdfunding campaign. Plus, these platforms are more productive if a bigger percentage of the audience can be a customer (versus, for example, the 2 percent of the U.S. population dealing with palmm's beachhead indication; Doolittle et al. 2016). I once participated in an informative session on how to prepare for these campaigns and was surprised to learn that you should expect to spend up to 30 percent of the funds raised on platform fees and the campaign itself (for an interesting discussion of this topic, see also www.launchboom.com/crowdfunding-guides/how-much-does-a-kickstarter-campaign-cost-updated/). So, whenever you hear someone has raised $100,000 through Kickstarter, you can expect that resulted in about $70,000 in available funds. Still, if you do raise successfully, this can be an effective marketing tactic.

### When to Engage

You should consider collaborators and customers as potential sources of funding at any time in the life of your startup, keeping the caveats called out above in mind. It's this type of out-of-the-box thinking that can result in unique opportunities for scrappy entrepreneurs.

# 9. Venture Capital

Of all types of funding sources, most of what has been said and written about is VC, so it shouldn't be too hard to find resources to help you on this topic. An excellent reference is *Venture Deals* (Mendelson and Feld 2019). It offers an enlightening peek into the venture capitalist's mind, with a lot of detailed info to help you understand term sheets, cap tables, and other topics that you'll get to deal with when you raise money from VCs and other investors. Here, I'll add just a few nuggets that I found particularly helpful while interacting with VC firms.

First off, venture capitalists are middlemen. They raise their funds from *limited partners* (LPs), who give them the power to invest those funds as best as they can. Their goal is to achieve a minimum return on investment (ROI) after a given amount of time (e.g., 5 times the original investment after 5-7 years could be a desired ROI in medtech). This implies that VCs work in cycles: Sometimes they have fresh money and are actively looking to invest it. At other moments, they are fundraising themselves, looking to convince their LPs that they have done a good job and should get more funds to invest in other companies.

Note that many of the insights called out in this section for VCs also apply to Family Offices, advisory firms that handle investments for affluent families. One key difference is that Family Offices do not operate on a set investment cycle. Their perspective is typically longer term.

### Pros and Cons

The assets a VC firm has under its management, referred to as AUM (assets under management), can range from a few million to billions of dollars. The average check size you can expect scales with that AUM. For

VCs with a lower AUM, a small exit with a decent multiple may be worth it. VCs with a very high AUM want to put more capital at work per investment to keep the number of portfolio companies manageable and for a chance to be a bigger part of a major success story. Ask for a VC's AUM, and more specifically the size of their current fund, so that you know whether your ideal check size is within the range that the VC is willing to spend per portfolio company.

VC firms typically set aside funds for their portfolio companies beyond that initial check, so that they can *follow on* in future funding rounds. This is beneficial to you if they invest in you, as that will make it easier to raise your next rounds of funding.

VC funding is dilutive, and negotiation of the deal terms is a must. See *Venture Deals* (Mendelson and Feld 2019) for more details on this topic.

### When to Engage

Some VC firms may bite with just a solid idea and a strong team, while others will be looking for business traction. Generally, VC firms have a statement about investment focus on their website. To get an even clearer idea, you can research their investment portfolio to understand how they have applied that theory in the past. Websites such as Crunchbase and PitchBook can be informative in this regard.

In *Startup Myths and Models*, Rizwan Virk writes:

> … in my experience with fundraising efforts over the years, there were two conditions that made it more likely than not that a VC would invest. …
>
> 1. The investor was *already* predisposed to invest in the market that I was in.
> 2. There was some previous connection to the investor (either I knew them, or one of my advisers or existing investors knew them, or they were connected to my alma mater, etc.).
>
> (Virk 2020)

This viewpoint might seem a bit pessimistic as it may seem like you have no control over these conditions. However, it does provide insight into when is the right time to engage with which VCs. With regard to condition (1), it is crucial to find VCs that are truly interested in what you are doing. And because there is not an endless pool of investors, it pays off to do that research ahead of time and be really targeted (as Virk also mentions in the book).

Condition (2) underscores the need for entrepreneurs to continue to invest in their network. But even if you don't have common connections, you can aim to socialize with people active in the VC world well before you want money from certain VCs so that you'll be on their *known* list when you do need money. Say hello at a reception and try to make a personal connection. Don't go into selling mode (maybe even avoid talking about work?)—just make sure they start establishing memories. Once you have gotten funding through other routes and are ready to raise VC funding, they'll have known you for a year or two already.

### Resources to Find VCs

Finding relevant VCs is as hard as finding any other type of investor. The types of websites that I mentioned above (Crunchbase, Pitchbook) can be helpful. I spent hours looking for companies that seemed broadly similar to what we were doing at palmm (i.e., medtech companies, companies focused on dermatology, companies with a bioelectronics technology, etc.) and then mapping out their investor base to add to our list of potential investor targets.

# 10. Strategic Companies

Companies that are potential acquirers of your technology may be willing to make an early investment. They generally do this with the main objective of staying close to relevant technologies in development.

### Pros and Cons

Getting a strategic on your cap table sends an important signal to outsiders that the opportunity you are pursuing is real. It therefore may make it easier to attract additional investments from other funding sources. Another plus is that you get to build a relationship with a potential acquirer.

From an accounting perspective, it is beneficial for the strategic to invest an amount that does not give them significant ownership. Specifically, they should own less than 20 percent of your company stock to avoid having to include the startup's profits and losses (P&L) in their earnings report (*Chron Contributor* 2020). This may be a consideration for them in negotiations relating to check size and valuation. If they are willing to invest $2 million, then it will be more attractive to do that in a company that is worth at least $10 million.

If a strategic decides to make an early investment, they often want special rights as part of the deal to have an edge over their competitors when it comes to acquiring you. A typical term is a *right of first refusal*, lawyer-speak for getting first dibs to acquire further down the line. Strategics may also want to start aligning some of your business processes with theirs for an easier potential acquisition. For example, if you have a less sophisticated document control system, they may want you to upgrade. Or they may prefer certain vendors over others for key activities. This may end up slowing you down and, potentially, even complicate an acquisition by an alternative strategic as they may prefer different business processes. If a strategic has such demands, make sure to assess pros and cons. I know of two medtech companies who were in this situation, and one of them got burned by it: They were slowed down significantly by the alignment of processes, and, when their technology was ready to be acquired, the strategic was going through a reorganization and decided to divest this part of their business, meaning they were no longer interested in acquisition. The result—all the effort to align processes was a waste.

Some entrepreneurs are afraid to engage with strategics for the risk of getting their ideas stolen. In my opinion, that risk is small for the majority of innovation-driven startups even though there may be industry-specific nuances. For big companies, it takes a lot to start a new project anyways, and the risk for them if they are accused of copying ideas is big. That said, it is not impossible. Having initial IP filed before you reach out is obviously a must. Other than that, it's a bit of a personal choice between remaining under the radar to minimize that risk versus reaching out to strategics to maximize your chances of getting funded.

*When to Engage*

Some established companies have an incubator or venture arm through which they make strategic investments (e.g., Johnson & Johnson, Intuitive Surgical, Unilever), while other companies may make these decisions as a one-off. Generally, if the strategic company has an incubator or venture arm, they are pretty transparent about their scope, similar to VCs. For others, my recommendation would be to get to know people within these strategic companies over time, without diving into the specifics of your company—similar to my recommendation for VC engagement.

*Resources to Find Strategics That Might Invest Early*

If you have done your market research, you will already know who the dominant players in your industry are. Who among them might be willing to invest earlier is a trickier question.

As I alluded to at the beginning of this chapter, I approached a strategic in the dermatology space very early on with palmm. They owned an incubator, but it was focused on digital health. I thought that we could convince them to go beyond digital health into medtech. It didn't pan out. In hindsight, it was probably too far of a stretch for them and not the right use of our time. We came across another strategic that had a venture arm, but they were focused on aesthetic dermatology. Some aesthetic dermatologists do treat excessive sweating, but if a patient approaches a dermatologist about this issue, it would typically be a general dermatologist (and 50 percent of people who have hand-sweat issues never talk about it with a physician at all). We decided not to engage with the aesthetic dermatology strategic at that time, and I'm glad we were able to spend our time on more fruitful activities. In summary, fit is key with identifying potential strategic investors. If you don't find the right one, waiting a bit longer before exploring this path further can be the best strategy.

## 11. Mixing and Matching Funding Types

Where your startup ends up getting its first money from depends on many factors, including the market size your idea addresses, general investor interest in the topic, your team, the amount of money you need, and, perhaps, some luck in meeting the right person at the right time. I recommend laying out your options, assessing the fit for your company stage, and then allocating your time accordingly across funding types. Take some meetings outside of what you think is optimal, so that you continue to learn and will see a pattern emerge if an alternative strategy has a lower path of resistance.

# CHAPTER 2

# What to Prepare

When it comes to preparing fundraising conversations, everyone focuses on the pitch deck, the first document that you present to new potential investors. But what else do innovation-driven startup founders need to have ready? Prior to kicking off palmm's fundraising efforts, I naively thought that I would just be answering questions as they came in after the initial conversation. When an angel group told me that they wanted to go into diligence, they did indeed have a few specific questions for me, but they also asked to gain access to our *data room*. I said yes, as I had a feeling it was something I should know. When the call ended, however, I quickly turned to my incubator neighbors: A data room, what was that? No one had asked me for this before, even though we had already received a few checks from individual angels by that time. Luckily, my fellow entrepreneurs were able to explain to me that a data room is simply a digital folder that contains more details on the various aspects of a company, such as key reference papers, results of market research, clinical studies, and so on.

To help you minimize the number of surprises like this one, let's go over what you should prepare for fundraising. We'll talk not only about elevator pitches, pitch decks, executive summaries, and data rooms but also about other things you'll want to research and set up upfront. We'll end with some reflections on the fundraising mindset.

## 1. Elevator Pitch

An elevator pitch is a very brief introduction of your company, designed to make the listener intrigued to learn more. Every startup, well-funded or not, needs one, so it won't be hard to find info on how to write yours. When it comes to delivery, practice makes perfect.

# 2. Pitch Deck

As with elevator pitches, it's easy to find tons of tips on how to put together a pitch deck on the web, but it can be hard to know which tips are worth paying attention to. And pitch decks can look vastly different depending on the industry and startup stage.

At the bare minimum, your pitch deck should include (a) an introduction of the unmet need your company aims to address, (b) a description of your proposed solution, (c) the resulting market opportunity, (d) an introduction to the team, and (e) the *ask* to your audience. I'll assume that you're the expert on the unmet need and your solution to it, so let's skip those here. Instead, we can go over what to keep in mind when crafting the market opportunity and the ask, and we'll devote the entire following section of this book to team-related considerations. I also have a few do's and don'ts for you in the present chapter regarding pitch deck layout and sharing your pitch document.

### Market Opportunity

The size of your addressable market should be one of the key considerations that helps you decide whether or not to pursue a business idea. Market sizing is a topic that I am passionate about and, for multiple years, I have taught palmm's approach to it in a graduate class at Stanford University. This book's online toolkit includes a template you can use for top-down and bottom-up calculations as part of a financial model (see page 53 for details on how to access the toolkit).

At palmm, my initial inclination was to include my most realistic, conservative assessment of the market size in my pitch decks. To my surprise, the feedback I received was different. Investor audiences typically assume that a founder's assessment is inherently inflated. A mentor who was also a professional investor flat-out told me that she would discount the numbers on the market opportunity slide by 25 to 50 percent regardless of the voiceover. Essentially, if I put $100 million on the slide, they would make $50 to 75 million out of it and dismiss the opportunity as too small. That said, if you project too large of a market, you will also appear uninformed. For example, in the medtech industry there are not a lot of products that reach *blockbuster* status (i.e., more than $1 billion in annual gross sales in the United States). If you are addressing a niche market and you project a multibillion-dollar opportunity, you will give the impression that you don't know what you're talking about.

With all this in mind, my recommendation is to come up with a reasonable and sufficiently optimistic estimate of the total/serviceable addressable market, verify that your numbers seem attractive enough for your industry, and then document your rationale and sources. I personally really like seeing footnotes with credible references on this slide to help instill a minimum level of confidence. Also be clear whether the opportunity that you display is a lifetime opportunity or an annual opportunity (in the latter case, call this out on the slide as your numbers will appear lower), and the geography to which it applies.

### The Ask

During your initial presentation you'll need to clarify your ask: What milestones do you want to hit next? How much funding do you need in order to achieve them? And what is the envisioned timeline to get there? Each of these three aspects is critical and takes time to put together—don't gloss over this. I love listening to the "How I Built This" podcast by former NPR journalist Guy Raz, as I always find the entrepreneurial stories inspiring. However, whenever I hear an entrepreneur on the show say something along the lines of "we didn't have a plan at all," I chuckle. In my experience, it doesn't work that way, at least not for first-time entrepreneurs in the medical device industry where you need a significant amount of funding before you can start selling your product.

There are certain milestones that investors like to pay for, while other milestones are necessary but not considered attractive inflection points for the company's value. Which are which will be highly dependent on your industry and even on the specific market and technology. For some projects, product development–related milestones can be used (as successful medtech entrepreneur Surbhi Sarna [2003] describes in her book *Without a Doubt*); however, for palmm, we learned that no one was willing to pay for just those. Even though from our perspective certain R&D aspects were critical, nontrivial activities, investors didn't expect our valuation would significantly increase by achieving those milestones, especially because they believed market adoption would be the biggest hurdle to overcome. Early milestones that typically are valued highly for medical devices are the completion of clinical trials, getting the green light from the FDA, and commercialization with a certain revenue/profit-related goal. As mentioned before, all of this depends on the project you're working on.

Once you know what milestones you'd like to achieve, you can estimate how much money your plan will require. As I described in the palmm example at the start of Chapter 1, you can plot your future path in multiple ways, with different target milestones and even differences in how lean or how fast you want to go. You should always add in a buffer to ensure that you have runway to finalize your next funding round after completing the planned milestones and to cover unforeseen delays. This is not often called out proactively, but through trial and error I learned that 6 to 9 months' worth of fixed costs can be added without getting strange looks. The model to calculate all this gets complex quickly, and there are a lot of parameters that you'll need. This book's toolkit includes a template you can use, based on what I put together for palmm (see page 53 for details on how to access the toolkit). It will be most appropriate for medtech companies, but it can also serve as a starting point for innovation-driven startups in other sectors. It took me multiple iterations to get to this version, which is both comprehensive enough to be useful and understandable at first sight for potential investors. A few of my entrepreneur friends have happily leveraged it for their ventures.

Back in 2019, when we set out to raise our second round for palmm, I had calculated that we needed $4 million to develop our product and get the green light from the FDA to start selling. This included about 9 months of additional runway and a 5 percent spending buffer for contingencies. When I shared this plan with mentors, I got feedback from a few of them that $4 million was not a good amount to ask for. It was too much for the angel (group) audience and too small for key VCs in our space. Initially I didn't know what to do with that feedback—until one mentor helped me think through which variables I could tweak to either need less money to reach a pared-down version of our target milestones or use more money to reach the market in a different way. That's how I decided to switch to a $2 million plan for the angel group and small VC audiences and a $15 million plan for larger VCs. The $2 million path

WHAT TO PREPARE     37

would race to FDA clearance with a small team, while the second plan would include a bigger team and more pre-commercial testing to achieve a stronger buy-in from the physician community from the get-go.

Another component of the *ask* is a simplified timeline of your development plan. The financial model shared above will give you the content. I always found it tricky to keep the accompanying slide simple yet sufficiently explanatory. Take a look at Figure 2.1 from a palmm pitch deck to see what I ended up with.

As you'll notice there, this timeline is in a way timeless: No months or years are on it. When presenting, you can voiceover dates, but I prefer to not write these on the slides directly. If you do want to give your audience a sense of the amount of time it will take to reach milestones, you can add that to your slide (e.g., by adding *x months* for each funding round). There are multiple advantages to doing it this way. First, it makes it easier for a listener or reader to gut-check proposed timelines. For example, how many months does it typically take to do this type of development work, or how long does it typically take to go through a given regulatory approval process? It also makes it easier for the potential investor to understand how long their money would be tied up if they decide to invest. Finally, it helps avoid hard links between milestones and actual dates. The reality depends on when and how much money you're able to get in—and you never have certainty on that. So, if I had spelled out that we would strive to obtain FDA clearance in Q2 2020 and we didn't achieve that goal, it would not reflect well on us when going back to those same investors later on (assuming they have digital copies that they can easily retrieve).

A final comment related to the ask is how to name your funding round. You'll hear entrepreneurs saying they're raising their *seed* round, a *series B* or even a *series seed* or a *series A-2*. It took me a while to realize that the definitions of these names aren't written in stone and that interpretations can differ by industry. Some say that you should only start naming rounds as *series* when you do a first priced round; any round before that (typically raised through convertible debt in the medtech industry) would be a *seed* round. With the letters, you can be sure that a series C round comes later than a series B round. But the company leadership could decide to sneak in a B-2 or bridge before moving on to C—for example, if they need a smaller amount of funding for some additional work prior to launching

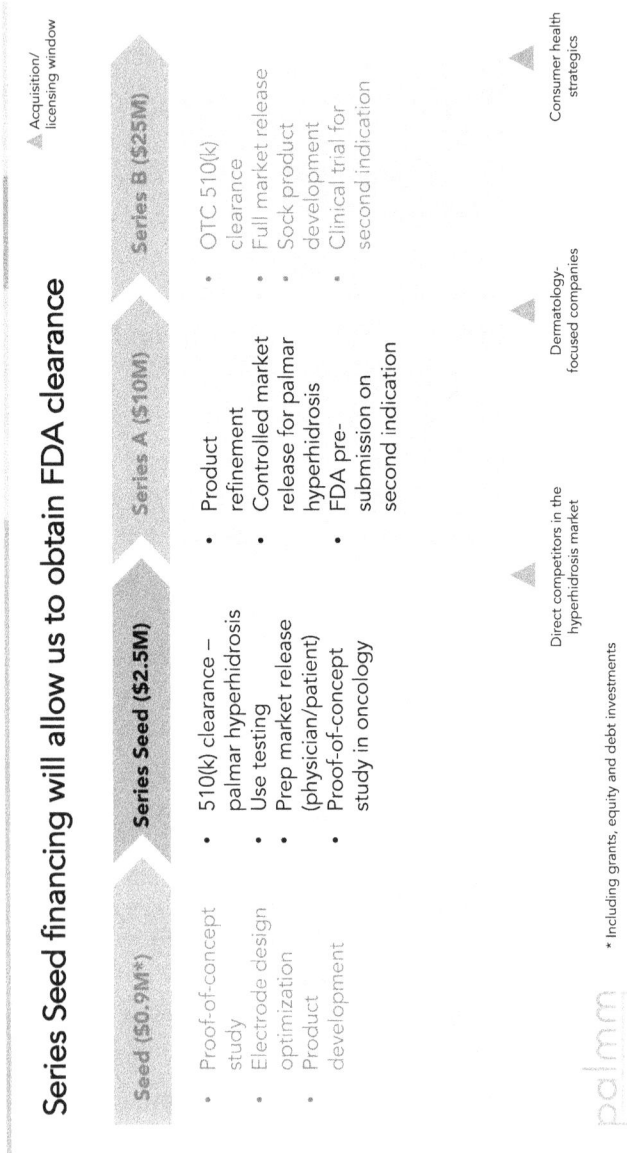

# Series Seed financing will allow us to obtain FDA clearance

**Seed ($0.9M*)**
- Proof-of-concept study
- Electrode design optimization
- Product development

**Series Seed ($2.5M)**
- 510(k) clearance – palmar hyperhidrosis
- Use testing
- Prep market release (physician/patient)
- Proof-of-concept study in oncology

**Series A ($10M)**
- Product refinement
- Controlled market release for palmar hyperhidrosis
- FDA pre-submission on second indication

**Series B ($25M)**
- OTC 510(k) clearance
- Full market release
- Sock product development
- Clinical trial for second indication

▲ Acquisition/licensing window

▲ Direct competitors in the hyperhidrosis market

▲ Dermatology-focused companies

▲ Consumer health strategics

palmm

* Including grants, equity and debt investments

*Figure 2.1  An example timeline slide from a palmm pitch deck (slightly adapted with permission from palmm Co.)*

the drive toward a bigger milestone. In medtech for devices that have a moderate risk to the patient, a series A round is often associated with clinical work, while series B and C rounds are more typically related to early commercialization. Later rounds can be about giving commercialization a further boost, expanding internationally, or adding to the product portfolio. Higher letters generally go hand in hand with bigger amounts raised, but as you go into the later letters (D, E, F, etc.), the amount may drop again. By the way, you'd hope that your company increases in value from one round to the next. If that is not the case, this is called a down-round.

To know what to call your round, get a sense of what is common in your industry or see if your savvy corporate attorney has a strong viewpoint on this.

### Pitch Deck Style

Go with a slide layout and style that you will feel comfortable presenting and that investors in your domain will like. The latter may differ by audience and even by geography. When I went to present for an angel group in Boston, I got a recommendation to add more commentary on my slides than I would typically include when presenting to groups in the San Francisco Bay Area.

I recently came across pitch.com and liked the slick examples provided there (https://pitch.com/presentations/collections/Pitch-Decks -7Kin4U5NYKdK4Zm7Do2SzzTC), even if these decks do seem a bit pared down. You can also take a look at Bestpitchdecks.com and Pitchenvy.com. While I prefer having full control over my pitch deck designs, I have seen other entrepreneurs successfully leverage support from creative platforms such as 99designs or Pitch Deck Creators.

### Sharing Your Pitch Deck

Many investors ask to have the presentation document e-mailed to them. Early on I would just send out the slides I had presented, in PDF format to prevent anyone on the receiving end from fiddling with them. Once I got introduced to DocSend (now part of Dropbox), I liked using that instead as it enabled me to check if the document had been opened, send targeted reminders as needed, and see what slides had been reviewed—all particularly helpful functionalities if you know the link is getting shared with an entire angel group or so.

When you share a deck, you should not hesitate to make it more reader-friendly than the version that you present live. There won't be any voiceover, so you want to guide the reader better. You can add more text and numbering, strategically add additional slides, or refer to an appendix slide to minimize the risk of misinterpretation.

# 3. The Initial Conversation

Every conversation with a potential investor is a unique chance to win them over. Effective storytelling gives you a leg up, as David Riemer will help you appreciate in *Get Your Startup Story Straight* (Riemer 2021). The conversation should not be a one-way street. For example, you also want to determine if they may be interested in your market and technology, if they have money available to spend, and if you trust them enough to enter into a business relationship with them. You should do some homework upfront so that you can ask the right questions during the meeting to gain clarity on all of these topics. Below are some particular nuances you'll want to explore in the initial conversation, arranged by funding type and including tips to help you in your background research:

## For Incubators/Accelerators

If there is a non-negligible cost to joining an incubator/accelerator, this needs to be weighed carefully relative to services offered. This is often easier said than done, as it can be hard to understand how valuable services are until you experience them. Take the time to question the incubator/accelerator staff and current and past companies-in-residence. You can get a sense of this upfront by browsing the incubator/accelerator's website.

## For Individual Angels

The key with individual angels is to have an enjoyable first conversation, so knowing the person's background and interests in advance is helpful. LinkedIn is a good starting point, combined with some separate searches

WHAT TO PREPARE    41

on the person's name and organizations with which they have been active. Look for common ground that you can bring up and allow this information to steer your pitch (e.g., someone who is deep into electronics may want to know more about that part of your technology). You want to stack all cards in your favor! For the conversation itself, you just want to get them excited about your idea. And then, whether it's in that initial conversation or a following one, you want to ask—in a convincing and passionate yet neutral way—if they'd like to be a part of the journey.

You want to avoid asking angels questions that can elicit an answer that shuts the door on you even before you have properly pitched to them, as it's hard to undo that. For example, in our first set of pitches to individual angel investors, I would ask upfront if the person was currently actively investing. That turned out to be a bad starting point, as it would often trigger a defensive gut reaction, thereby closing a door.

Once the conversation goes to funding, you can indicate that there is a minimum check size. This helps to keep the cap table manageable, meaning fewer people to reach out to and less chance of someone disagreeing further down the line. For palmm's first round, I set a minimum check size of $50,000. This ended up making two candidate investors increase their proposed investment amount to match that threshold.

As an aside, if you are not a solo founder, you may wonder if all cofounders need to be present for a pitch. I have found that that is not needed. Ideally the CEO takes the lead, while other cofounders move different aspects of the business forward. They can then join a later conversation to share their expertise.

### For Angel Groups

After your first conversation with an angel group member, you should be familiar with their investment focus (i.e., what they like to invest in), their investment model (i.e., investing together or separately, amount of capital in the fund if there is one), and their investment process (i.e., what steps do entrepreneurs need to go through). Learn upfront by assessing their past portfolio. Knowing the group's typical check size will be helpful too. As mentioned in the previous section on individual angels, setting a minimum check size is common practice. However, these company-set minima can be a barrier for angel groups where check sizes by individual may be lower. You can consider allowing a lower individual check size for angel group members to circumvent this issue.

I would personally avoid getting into a conversation about deal terms early on. But if that's where they go, you should be able to respond. The most common terms that get discussed for a convertible note round (the typical vehicle for a first funding round) are the company valuation cap, discount rate, and interest rate. You can easily find those terms explained on the web (see, for example, https://spzlegal.com/blog/funding/important -terms-convertible-note-convertible-equity). When we raised our first round, a valuation cap of somewhere between $4 million and $8 million was typical for early-stage medtech companies. (Quite a bit higher than the maximum valuation that the Berkus method,[6] which you might hear about in business class, suggests!) We placed our valuation cap in the middle of that range. A discount rate of 20 percent and an interest rate of 6 percent were typical according to our attorney and peers, and we chose not to do anything out of the ordinary.

Another topic that angel groups and other investors may have on their mind is the company's exit strategy, as this is how they will ultimately get money back. Do you expect to get acquired, or is an Initial Public Offering (IPO) more likely? If the former, you should be able to name a few potential acquirers of your technology. Ideally you can reference three or more comparable companies that had recent successful exits. You should know how much investment went into them and their valuation at acquisition or IPO.

### For VCs

Similar to angel groups, you want to make sure that you understand a VC's investment process and have a very clear idea of their investment thesis. It's also important to understand what stage the fund is at: Do they have money they can invest (and, if so, how much?), or are they in the process of raising their own money from limited partners (as per the *Venture Capital* section on page 26)? VCs don't often seem to offer this info up proactively, even though it really helps to understand whether they would be able to invest quickly if they wanted to. If you will run out of funds in a few months, and they aren't ready to spend anywhere soon, this will help you focus your efforts on other investors.

What are their AUM, and how many investments do they plan on making (which together give you a sense of average check size)? How much do they set aside for follow-on investments? Have they had any recent exits that make them want to (re)invest available funds quickly? Make sure to research their past and existing portfolio companies to have more informed questions for your conversation.

### For Strategic Companies

If the strategic company you're meeting has an incubator or VC arm, your questions will be very similar to what you can find above for those categories. If they don't, you want to make sure you understand if they at least have experience making early-stage investments. This might not be available on the company website, so you should ask for any information they are able to share with you on that front. Your chances of success are slimmer if they do not have any experience here.

## 4. Executive Summary

When a mentor suggested I put together an executive summary, I was a bit surprised. An executive summary is one to two pages long and describes the key aspects of your company. Like any other fundraising materials you create, it should be clear and compelling. I was surprised there was a need for such a document, as I had previously always sent a pitch deck whenever someone asked me for a high-level introduction to the company. Still, once I had created the document that is reproduced in Figure 2.2, it was an asset that I used quite a bit. It does take a good amount of work to get it right, and, of course, it is yet another document that you need to keep current. But when you're fundraising, you have to cater to your audience. Our attorney also asked us to include this document as part of the paperwork that went with the convertible note, so it got put to use again in this capacity.

## 5. Data Room

As per the introduction of this chapter, angel groups, VC firms, and strategic companies will ask you for access to your data room. See Figure 2.3

**Company**

palmm Co. is a pre-market therapeutic medical technology company, founded in 2017 and based at the Fogarty Institute for Innovation, a premier medtech incubator in Mountain View, CA. The company originated out of a Stanford Biodesign Innovation Fellowship project following the principles of need-driven innovation.

**Five reasons to invest**

✓ $4B US total addressable market

✓ Convenient, home-use product

✓ Clear 510(k) predicate

✓ Razor-razorblade business model

✓ Pipeline of products and indications

**Unmet need**

palmm's therapy can address unmet needs in dermatology, oncology, consumer skincare and sports. The company's initial focus is on hyperhidrosis, chronic excessive sweating, a dermatologic issue that can have a dramatic impact on quality of life. The condition affects 15M Americans and is even more prevalent in the Asian population. Treatment options available today – including antiperspirants, drugs and botulinum toxin injections – can be ineffective, inconvenient, invasive and/or expensive. palmm's first product focuses on hand sweat, with a product pipeline to treat other anatomical sites. Another application of interest is the management of sweat-related chemotherapy side effects. palmm's total addressable market opportunity is estimated at $4B in the US alone.

**Product**

*palmm's first product: e-antiperspirant in a glove*

palmm's first product is a pair of gloves, with integrated power pod and multi-use glove liner, that delivers low-level electrical energy to treat palmar hyperhidrosis. The company leverages an existing mechanism of action combined with state-of-the-art wearable electronics. Patients wear the gloves for just 20-30 minutes, once weekly on an ongoing basis, to keep hands dry. The same principles will be applied to treating other body parts through this safe, effective and convenient therapy.

The company has one issued utility patent, and additional patents pending (US and international), covering the core technology and embodiments that will allow treatment of other anatomical sites and indications.

**Status**

A proof-of-concept study conducted with 11 palmar hyperhidrosis patients demonstrated a marked and controllable reduction in sweat levels of 59%±16% after two weeks of treatment.

**Go-to-market strategy**

palmm will leverage a razor-razorblade business model, at a price point acceptable for out-of-pocket purchase. After obtaining regulatory clearance (510(k) with clear predicate),

**Financing**

The company is seeking Series A financing of up to $15M to achieve the following milestones:

- FDA clearance (palmar hyperhidrosis)
- User testing for marketing purposes
- Voice of customer program in preparation of a controlled market release
- Proof-of-concept study in oncology

palmm will gain clinical credibility in a controlled release in close collaboration with key dermatologists. Sales for this product can be scaled further by leveraging online marketing channels to drive user demand.

**Team**

*Véronique Peiffer, PhD, CEO*: Former Manager McKinsey & Company, Biodesign '15-'16
Experienced R&D team (incl. former Miramar Labs/miraDry, Auris Health)
*Advisors* include Patricia Altavilla (Suneva Medical, Zeltiq, Merz Aesthetics), Frederick Duffy Jr., MD (Texas Plastic Surgery Associates), Matt Davidson, PhD (Verrica Pharmaceuticals), Fogarty Institute for Innovation

*Figure 2.2 palmm's executive summary (slightly adapted with permission from palmm Co.)*

for the folder structure that I set up for palmm's data room based on examples from my incubator neighbors. Some folders in this structure are clearly industry-specific, such as the need for a home for clinical-related documents in a health care company.

We used Dropbox for filekeeping, so that's where our data room was housed as well. Sharing with investors through Dropbox (or Box, Google Drive, or another similar software) allows you to expire the shareable link and gives you further control of access, which is helpful to avoid over-sharing of your company's information.

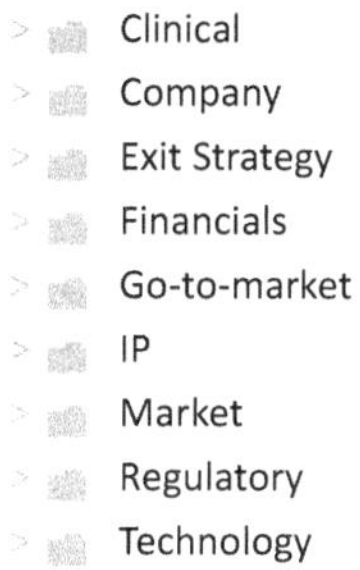

> Clinical
> Company
> Exit Strategy
> Financials
> Go-to-market
> IP
> Market
> Regulatory
> Technology

*Figure 2.3  An example startup folder structure (with permission from palmm Co.)*

# 6. Follow-up Interactions

For follow-up interactions with investors, it is important to be able to demonstrate that you're making progress. Ideally, you can say that you're focusing on element X of your startup, and 1 to 3 months later, demonstrate that you have been able to do exactly what you said you were going to do. This can be hard, as you probably have a million things going on in parallel, and it's easy to lose track of what you said to whom. Sometimes you're also just not able to achieve what you thought you would. If you can plan it out to make sure you always have one to two new updates in the months after you meet with a new investor, they'll be impressed. This can involve anything, from hiring (in the broadest sense of the term) to product updates, to strategy, funding, or IP. Anything really, as long as it can help show drive and momentum. You want to generate some level of FOMO.

Well-executed demos are typically impactful. But even simple product mockups can be effective for innovation-driven startups where it takes time and money to get to the actual product. Inside everyone, including investors, is a child who likes to play with toys. A visual representation or physical object is memorable and enlivens the conversation. I sometimes liked to keep the demo or mockup for a follow-up conversation to increase the level of excitement.

Some founders write monthly newsletters to provide these types of updates and send them out to everyone they have interacted with. I am personally not a fan of this for tiny startups: It creates pressure on fronts where you don't need it, and it's easy for such e-mails to get forwarded to anyone—including your competitors. Some entrepreneurs also put occasional exciting news updates on their website or on LinkedIn. That is in itself fine. Just keep in mind that you should keep doing it once you've started. If you had regular updates till 2 years ago and then nothing since on your platform, it may give the impression that you have lost momentum.

When you get a yes from an investor, the answer you have been dying to hear, work fast! Send documents over as soon as you can, and don't hesitate to touch base with them weekly until you have everything you need. Doing so, I never had an investor change their mind—but I have certainly heard about such scenarios playing out elsewhere.

## From Another Perspective: Tailoring Your Message to the Investor

If there is any entrepreneur who has impressed me with their know-how and tenacity, it is Gabriel Sanchez. Gabriel is cofounder and CEO of Enspectra Health, a medtech company poised to redefine how disease is diagnosed by leveraging revolutionary imaging and machine learning algorithms. They recently received the go-ahead from the FDA to start commercializing their platform VIO™ System, a major accomplishment for a technology that was only being studied in a research setting when Gabriel and his cofounders started their work to translate the idea from the university into the clinical setting.

Gabriel has raised millions of dollars in investment from a combination of angel investors and early-stage venture funds (in addition to a similar amount in grant funding). He is adamant that warm intros are a must.

People invest in people they know, so you're always looking for your personal contacts to introduce you to their connections. And then, your new connections need to get to know you over time. Angel investors who invest independently, not as part of an angel group, may invest based on social or environmental impact, personal values, or personal experience. Before talking with a potential angel investor, I always do my research, so that I can tailor my message to what I believe may excite them most. I also like to have these conversations in person over a coffee, so that we can get to know each other. I was lucky not to have to do any fundraising from angels in the COVID/Zoom era, as that would have been much trickier. I am convinced that the first five minutes of the initial conversation matter most, although it typically still takes a handful of meetings to close a deal. With angel groups, all of this gets even trickier: There are a lot of opinions around the table, so there will be lots of reasons to turn you down. Angel groups also often have a fairly formal diligence process, even for relatively modest investments. This is why I quickly shifted my focus to early-stage venture funds. These invest purely on the economics, so the story to highlight sounds very different from what you discuss with individual angels. While you should tailor angel conversations individually, venture funds will want to hear about the potential for a sizeable return on investment early on.

When I asked Gabriel which referrals are not helpful, his thoughts went to the investor's investment thesis.

In some cases, you just aren't the right fit. If you do your research upfront, you'll know if their sweet spot is simply different from what you're focused on. In those instances, you have to decide how you balance your time. Sometimes, I still take those meetings, but with the goal of expanding my network, as it may eventually lead me to a new successful warm intro.

## 7. Keeping Track of It All

One aspect of startup life that I had not imagined would take as much time and effort as it does is bookkeeping, and it is required on multiple fronts, including fundraising. The more people you talk with, the easier it is to lose track. And losing track means that there is a chance you are the one dropping the ball, wasting an opportunity to strengthen a connection. Over the years, I have refined a spreadsheet tracker that maintains a list of who I have been in touch with. It contains information on the potential investor, the person who introduced you to this contact, the conversation stage, and the next steps. It is included in the Scrappy Entrepreneur's toolkit (see page 53 for details on how to access this toolkit). Alternative options are tools like Trello or Asana, or keeping notes on your phone's contacts app. In addition to these notes, you want to make sure you don't forget to take the next step, 1 or 2 weeks after a conversation. While I didn't use it at the time, Google Tasks could be a great tool for this. You could also work with calendar reminders or a separate document that you refer to every morning.

As you can see in the template that I introduced above, I also like to keep notes on key topics discussed. You could just do this on paper, but doing it in a digital format—whether in Excel or Word or through a more specific notes-taking option (OneNote, Evernote, Google Keep, etc.)—has the advantage of being more organized and searchable. You can also keep a log of questions asked and the best answer to those. This will help you better prepare for next conversations and even sync answers across team members when needed. This tracking exercise can become cumbersome, so design a method that works for you. Just to clarify, the frequently asked questions (FAQ) I mentioned should be a document for internal use. I would never recommend sharing an extensive FAQ externally. You don't want to have potential investors asking a whole new set of questions just because someone else asked them. Startup life is already busy enough!

## 8. Fundraising Flair

Fundraising takes a certain mindset. The process is much easier if you can stay calm, be optimistic, and even have fun. In short: Don't worry, be happy!

Coming across in a calm and relaxed manner has advantages beyond just feeling better. The more confident you seem about the whole process, the more convinced interested parties will be that you can tackle anything.

Being optimistic is the second key trait of the successful fundraiser. Never indicate that you will ever consider shutting down the company. When Justin and I got started, we thought investors would think of us as smart if we explained what might kill the project, if asked. But ultimately most investors don't want to invest in someone who is this reasonable. They'd rather invest in someone who is passionate and determined and will never give up, no matter what happens. If, from the beginning, you indicate that things may go south and that that will be the end of it, they're more likely to hedge their bets.

Also, have fun with it. You'll meet lots of interesting individuals. During my fundraising journey with palmm, I met many people who I have truly enjoyed interacting with. As a result, the range of individuals who ended up investing in palmm was broad: from a young person who got rich with an early fintech exit to someone in their 80s with tons of relevant experience and intriguing stories. If you focus on enjoying the interactions, you can let the origin of your first check be a pleasant surprise.

Lastly, to help achieve a positive fundraising mindset, I find tremendous value in connecting with other startup CEOs. At Fogarty Innovation, I instituted a monthly CEO-only meeting to discuss our wins and struggles and to vent, celebrate, and exchange learnings. Hearing other people's perspectives on fundraising gives you a more balanced viewpoint. I was reminded of that when listening to the stories from my fellow entrepreneurs in the process of writing this book. I'm sure that you'll agree with me on this when you read the *From Another Perspective* section below.

Fogarty Innovation also has a leadership coach on staff. Working with her to check in on my mental state on a regular basis was tremendously helpful to recognize and avoid trigger points.

## From Another Perspective: Fundraising Without Guilt

While my general advice for fundraising is to be positive, that is sometimes easier said than done. When I asked other entrepreneurs what they considered to be the hardest part of startup life, this issue often bubbled up to the top. Bronwyn Harris, who cofounded Tueo Health (a company focused on controlling childhood asthma) and led it to its successful exit, reflected:

I had never taken money from anyone, so asking individuals for $25,000 felt like a big deal—and it is. But looking back,

I should have felt less stressed about it. It would have helped me to take guilt out of the equation. As long as you only take money from those who can afford it, they will understand the risk and not be in trouble if you cannot return the money.

Similarly, Maria Aboytes, who developed a medical technology for treating brain aneurysms and sold her company, Medina Medical, to Medtronic (one of the largest medical device companies globally) in 2015, also felt that early fundraising was the hardest part of first-time entrepreneurship. Describing raising the first $50,000, Maria recalled,

I didn't feel comfortable asking others for help. I felt like I was asking for charity. So, I asked people I used to work with and who I knew were financially in a good spot. I started with $10,000 here, $20,000 there. And then one time at a con-ference, I met a business development person from Covidien (which later became Medtronic) who was interested in what I was doing. She sent her R&D counterpart to come see our bench-top model. They ended up investing $1 million, which really got us going.

# CHAPTER 3

# Key Takeaways from Part 1—Fundraising

## ☼ Key Learnings

1. At any stage in the life of your startup, keep in mind that there are multiple potential funding sources. Every 6 months, reassess which ones have the highest chances of success for you, leveraging Table 1.1 as a guide.
2. Have a few grant applications in the pipeline for as long as you consider your company to be underfunded.
3. To identify the best timing to pitch a particular angel group, VC firm, or strategic company, investigate when they initially invested in their existing portfolio companies.
4. Not every introduction to a new potential investor is equal. The best introductions come from fellow entrepreneurs and your active investors.
5. To increase your chances of obtaining funding from an angel group, get an influential *insider* to commit to investing prior to your official presentation and prepare a plan to demonstrate traction in the 6 months after your official presentation.
6. Steer away from family and friends as investors.
7. Ask a VC about their AUM so that you know whether your ideal check size is within the range that they are willing to spend per portfolio company.
8. Don't disregard collaborators, future customers, and strategic companies in your industry as potential sources of funding.
9. For a new funding round, don't be afraid to try out two pitch decks in parallel, with different plans, projected milestones, and related asks. This will enable you to best meet the appetite of each investor

candidate with whom you engage. Once you identify a first investor for either of these plans, you should, of course, march forward with just a single plan.

10. Consider what milestones each investor type will be excited to fund when determining an appropriate *ask*.

11. Include an additional 6 to 9 months of runway in your funding ask to give your future self time to complete your next raise and as a buffer for unforeseen delays.

12. Don't use dates in projected timelines. Instead, use *round closed* as your t = 0 and build the timeline out from there.

13. Adapt your pitch deck to the delivery method: The written version can be different from the one you present, to help prevent misperceptions in the absence of your voiceover.

14. Be careful about how you send company documents to third parties, including potential investors. Tools such as DocSend can be helpful to protect your information and provide insight into how it was received.

15. Prepare a data room before you start pitching angel groups, VC firms, or strategic companies.

16. Have a perspective on your proposed deal terms, as well as your envisioned exit strategy. The most common deal terms that get discussed for a convertible note round (the typical vehicle for a first funding round) are the company valuation cap, discount rate, and interest rate.

17. Investor conversations should be a two-way street. Prepare questions that will help you gauge your likelihood of getting money from them and whether these individuals will be the right fit for you.

18. Demos can be particularly impactful in follow-on conversations.

19. Don't be the one to drop the ball on an interaction with a potential investor. Use tools to help you with reminders and log conversation topics.

20. Don't say you'll ever consider shutting down the company.

21. Don't forget to enjoy the many fun aspects of the fundraising process!

# Key Tools and Resources Provided

- Helpful references for information related to (U.S.) patents: The USPTO's Patent Center (https://patentcenter.uspto.gov) and Google Patents (https://patents.google.com)
- List of pitch competitions and grant opportunities, focused on cash-awarding opportunities in the United States: Included in the Scrappy Entrepreneur's toolkit
- List of angel groups: https://angelcapitalassociation.org/directory/
- Resources that can help you understand an investor's past investment behavior: Crunchbase (www.crunchbase.com) and Pitchbook (www.pitchbook.com)
- Financial model template including market sizing calculations: Included in the Scrappy Entrepreneur's toolkit (In the document, see tabs following the "Revenues =>" tab)
- Discussion on the topic of cost of crowdfunding campaigns: www.launchboom.com/crowdfunding-guides/ how-much-does-a-kickstarter-campaign-cost-updated/
- Pitch slide deck examples: Pitch.com, Bestpitchdecks.com, Pitchenvy.com
- Explanation of key terms related to convertible notes and convertible equity: https://spzlegal.com/blog/funding/ important-terms-convertible-note-convertible-equity
- Investor tracker template: Included in the Scrappy Entrepreneur's toolkit
- Helpful reference for legal aspects of starting a business: www. CooleyGO.com

Note: Visit veroniquepeiffer.com to receive a copy of the Scrappy Entrepreneur's toolkit.

# PART 2

# Team

Building out and managing a team is among the most rewarding, but also one of the hardest, aspects of startup life—particularly for scrappy entrepreneurs. Why? First, there is the cost issue: You may have a vision of the ideal team, but this vision doesn't match the team you can afford today. Second, there is the *right person at the right time* issue. The best possible team you can afford today does not necessarily equal the team you will have, because you need to be able to find, hire, and retain these individuals. And third, there is the issue of unpredictability: Someone claims to be great at something, but the reality proves different; someone did really intend to do one thing, but then life changes and now that one thing doesn't match their desires anymore; and so on. There is nothing you can do to eliminate these three dynamics, but there are ways to minimize their impact—which we'll talk about in this section of the book. Even following this advice, hiring, managing, and retaining a team will never be a perfectly straight path.

## A Practical Example

We always had a small team with palmm. Read: We never had more than two employees on the payroll, up to a handful of part-time consultants, and, in later stages, two or three vendors we'd work with on a regular basis. Still, the list of anecdotes I have that involve team-related wins and losses seems endless. The most momentous event along these lines has to do with my cofounder Justin. We had been working on our business idea for roughly 2 years. We would check in regularly with each other to discuss how we felt about our progress and our excitement about our work overall. During one of these off-sites, Justin told me that he wanted to step out of his full-time role. We both saw that many important risks remained to be retired for palmm, and Justin knew that the equation

wasn't going to work for him. I was devastated! We had started researching excessive hand sweat because it was a problem Justin had been personally affected by for as long as he could remember. In every investor
conversation we had, no one ever doubted that Justin would continue
to be motivated to treat his own condition. If anything, people wanted
to know why I would stick with this project. But here we were with the
exact opposite scenario playing out. Talk about startup life being unpredictable! Justin's decision had multiple ramifications, but one of them
was that I needed to find someone to take over the lead on our R&D
efforts. As one of the founders, Justin had been a cost-effective resource
for us in directing these critical portions of our business. While I am
an engineer by training, I didn't have the know-how or skills to prototype the way he could. It was tricky to know what type of an engineer
I needed most to replace him. Our device hinged on electricity, so did
we need an electrical engineer? The electrical pieces would need to be
embedded in a glove, so was it better to find someone with experience
in the more nascent domain of wearables? We really needed someone
who could do all of the above, but where would I find someone like
that? Maybe it was time to finally engage one of the many vendors who
had approached us in the past, claiming they had all the skills in-house
to do what we needed and even wanting to invest in the company to
help lower our upfront cash needs. I had no other choice but to double
down on leveraging my network. I thought about companies that had
recently been acquired and who had worked there who might have relevant skillsets. Based on that information, I sent requests to second-degree
connections on LinkedIn and took a free membership upgrade so that
I could do cold outreaches where I wasn't able to connect directly. I sent
out about a dozen carefully crafted messages about why the recipient
should respond to a total stranger of an unknown startup by the name
of palmm, and this ended up leading to a handful of interesting conversations. Through this process, the type of expertise I really needed
became clear: Only those who had done early device prototyping as part
of a small team were able to think *out of the box* the way they needed to
for a company at our stage. They could be a mechanical engineer with
some high-level knowledge of electrical engineering, or the other way
round—but that prototyping savviness was key. I ended up gelling with

an electrical engineer whose previous employer had been acquired by a large health care company a couple of years prior. He had stuck with the acquirer to lead the next product iterations of their handheld electrical medical device. I asked one of my close mentors to interview him separately to check for blind spots on my side, and she agreed that he could be a great fit. I didn't have much competitive to offer him in terms of pay, but he was excited about the product we were developing. He agreed to moonlight with palmm 12 to 16 hours a week for a monthly retainer, plus some stock options vesting over 5 months.[7] He lived in Oakland, while our company was based in Mountain View, a 50-minute drive away even without traffic along one of the busiest highways in the San Francisco Bay Area. We made the effort to get together in person as often as possible. He would come over after his daytime job, we would meet in the middle, or I would drive up on Saturdays so we could look at his progress together. While I would have preferred Justin had continued to be an integral part of the team, bringing in a fresh perspective was a godsend in some ways. We had a few R&D breakthroughs thanks to him. However, I knew the collaboration was most likely a temporary one, as he had mentioned from the start that the distance wouldn't be manageable long term. During my search, a few other folks seemed like great candidates but weren't available for one reason or another. One of them was one of the key developers of the single technology to control excessive sweating that had made it to market over the past decade or so. This individual was probably the most knowledgeable engineer out there when it came to sweat glands, and he had early prototyping experience galore. His company had been acquired and he had left, but he had chosen to do a year of traveling and recharging. Justin and I had always felt like this engineer could be a great asset to our team, but we hadn't been able to engage given the potential conflict of interest.

When my first new R&D head had to move on, the sweat gland technology expert happened to be ready to start something else. Right person at the right time! Once again, the original disadvantage turned into an advantage, and the key intellectual property we developed at palmm was largely the fruit of his creative efforts.

Clearly, building out the team of a scrappy startup is a road full of adventures, involving both growing the team and managing voluntary and involuntary attrition. Those are the topics we'll devote the following three chapters to (Chapter 4 through Chapter 6). We'll also discuss how to talk about your team externally (Chapter 7), and close out this section of the book with some thoughts on how to cultivate a healthy team (Chapter 8). Let's talk about the founding team first as that's where it all begins.

# CHAPTER 4

# The Founding Team

We'll first touch on who makes up the founding team. We'll then consider the roles and titles of these individuals. And we'll go over how and how much they should compensate themselves.

## 1. Who Makes Up the Founding Team?

When it comes to appointing cofounders, there really shouldn't be a difference in approach between scrappy startups and any other early-stage company. Include those who are an instrumental part of the very early beginnings and are willing to take the risk to participate in the longer term. If an inventor does not plan to be involved in the future of the company, consider a licensing deal with a termination clause instead of including them as a founder. That way, you can end the agreement in case you decide to pivot.

As you look for cofounders, consider how you will work together as a founding team. After Justin had shared with me that he had been struggling with excessive hand sweat since childhood, we collaborated on analyzing this market opportunity and brainstorming solutions. Given we both had entrepreneurial aspirations and were passionate about the topic, it seemed only logical that we would move on to working together as cofounders. On top of this, Justin had two critical qualities that I felt were important as a cofounder: (1) He was relentless and hard-working and (2) we worked well together, thanks to complementary preferences and skillsets, so we were better together. We also knew each other pretty well from being housemates. I've seen some up-close examples of potential cofounders who did not know each other well, leading to unfortunate misalignments in expectations when it came to starting a business together.

## 2. Roles and Titles

Being a (co)founder is a title, not a role in a company. Deciding who will be the CEO and what titles other cofounders take is not always obvious, given that everyone typically does a bit of everything in a scrappy startup. Justin and I had many conversations about this. We felt that we could both make worthy CEOs. On the one hand, Justin was the one suffering from the problem we were treating, so making him the CEO would be a statement in and of itself. Additionally, and more important from a practical standpoint, Justin was by far the more extroverted of the two of us. He would get energized by networking events and keep talking, whereas I was ready to go home as soon as it was socially acceptable. He could be the better salesperson as a result, which is obviously important for fundraising—an activity that is typically led by the CEO. On the other hand, I had more business experience, coming from a strategic management consulting background with McKinsey & Company, which would be a plus in fundraising negotiations. Additionally, with me at the helm, there could be a tactical advantage of having a woman-led business. After many conversations on the topic, we agreed that Justin would take the CEO role for the reasons mentioned above, while I took the title of chief operating officer (COO). In our situation, there was no real downside either way. The key was making a decision we both felt good about and then running with it, which is what we were able to do.

I chose the COO title for myself, as I felt it reflected the more inward-facing tasks that I would focus on. Had Justin not been the CEO, he would probably have been the chief technology officer (CTO) given that he was leading R&D efforts. We both took *chief* titles to indicate to investors that we felt capable of leading those functions. If you don't think you'll lead a function in the longer run, you can opt for other titles, maybe *director*, *manager*, or *head of*, so that it will be easier to hire above you. These titles are a way to signal your intent, so make sure to utilize that opportunity. What you will be doing in those first months and even years is not going to be any different.

Note that I did end up becoming the CEO when Justin stepped back from the day-to-day operations. Despite being an introvert, the social aspect of the role grew on me over time.

# 3. Founder Compensation

One aspect we struggled with as founders was how to best compensate ourselves, given how strapped palmm was for cash. We would, of course, get shares in the company, but how about salaries?

Both Justin and I had had well-paid jobs in the past. When we started working for palmm, some potential investors claimed that we shouldn't compensate ourselves with cash as we were working for equity. In the expensive Silicon Valley that is literally impossible unless you have a bunch of money set aside. You'd have to take at least a side job that can pay the bills, which we steered away from for the most part as we preferred to be fully dedicated to this one endeavor. We ended up paying ourselves minimal wages and were really only able to get by that way because we didn't have families to take care of at the time. Thinking back on it, maybe we should have done it differently. We weren't valuing ourselves the way we should have. We could easily have been earning four-fold elsewhere in businesses with similar risk levels. Being content with a minimal salary may even have signaled to potential investors that we didn't have as much expertise as we really did have. Another entrepreneur told me that he used a different strategy. To begin with, he didn't want to start working for his startup full-time until the company had sufficient funds to pay him and his team decent salaries. In his business plans, he included his competitive salary, but he also indicated that he would only take that salary every other month. That way he clarified his real value to investors and, at the same time, confirmed that he didn't plan to burden the company with his own cost. A clever approach!

As I mentioned above, no one debated that we, as founders, should receive equity in the company. That said, the amount each cofounder receives needs to be agreed upon. Justin and I both felt that we were equal partners on this journey, so we granted ourselves the same number of *common shares*. Our corporate attorney wrote up the paperwork, also including an 18 percent option pool so that we would have that available for the next contributors. If you and your cofounders do not contribute equally to the company (e.g., your time spent toward the company's progress differs substantially or the type of contribution is significantly different between cofounders), you will have to think through the right split. There are various schools of thought on this topic, with a Harvard Business School article providing an interesting overview: https://startupguide.hbs.edu/people/founding-team/co-founder-equity-splits-ways-to-approach-allocations/.

As an aside, if the language of the last few sentences and the next ones seems like a foreign language to you, *Venture Deals* (Mendelson and Feld 2019) will make you feel very smart. Or you can search the web for *startup equity* to find short primers on the topic of startup corporate finance.

As is typical for startups these days, Justin and I agreed to have our shares vest over 4 years with a 1-year cliff.[8] Vesting shares is done to prevent a new contributor from receiving a bunch of shares and then immediately leaving the company. Such a scenario would result in dead equity.[5] While vesting over a period of 4 years is not a perfect solution, it is the method that is most widely accepted. If you do something different, you want to be clear about your rationale. A faster vesting clock may give the impression that you do not want to stick around. A slower clock may lead potential investors to believe that you think your progress will be below-average. Those potential perceptions lead most founders to decide to stick with what is common, rather than what is most logical. That's what Justin and I did as well.

# CHAPTER 5

# Growing the Team

As we're talking about *teams*, I want to clarify that I define the startup team broadly as consisting of more than just full-time employees. A scrappy startup can't afford to hire many full-time employees, so some critical contributors may not work for you full-time and may not be employees. They could be (part-time) consultants, vendors, incubator staff, mentors, advisers, and so on. All these individuals should know that they are truly part of your team, not just an extension of it.

Here is how palmm's project team grew over the first few months:

The first people to get involved beyond the cofounders were a handful of knowledgeable individuals in our network with whom we pressure-tested our business ideas. We also got some pro bono help from friendly attorneys, including a fellow Stanford Biodesign alum who helped us prepare our first provisional patent application.[9]

One collaborator we made a conscious effort to find early on was a relevant clinician. As we were working in the domain of dermatology, it was critical for us to get feedback on our product from practitioners in the field. We wanted at least one dermatologist to help us along the journey and to partner with us on clinical work. We spoke with multiple dermatologists and ended up building a great relationship with a clinical associate professor and practicing general dermatologist at Stanford Health Care.

On the other side of the experience spectrum, another early *hire* was a summer intern. We constantly felt strapped for time, so when we heard about a high school student who wanted to get some hands-on experience, we offered him that chance. For us, the additional hands were helpful to speed up our work.

Given the nature of our product and the lack of true electrical engineering know-how within our founding team, we pretty quickly onboarded an electrical engineering contractor to strengthen our team. But for various reasons it ended up taking us a number of tries and multiple years before we found the right hardware engineer and firmware engineer to support us for the longer term.

When we joined Fogarty Innovation we needed to incorporate our company, which prompted us to start a search for a corporate attorney. We wanted someone with experience in our field and preferred an independent attorney over a big firm, as we thought we would get more attention and right-sized advice. The person we found could not have been better.

Justin and I felt indebted to this early team for their support. They weren't full-time employees, but we felt that they were all proper team members. I remember that we organized a happy hour one day to thank them all together. Having everyone in the same room led to an unexpected advantage. It made everyone truly appreciate that they were part of something bigger and resulted in even deeper engagement.

In the section that follows, I'd like to give you a sense of what to keep in mind when you grow your team with various types of contributors.

## 1. Employees and Critical Consultants

When you're tight on money, I recommend having team members consult before you hire them as employees. It gives you a way to get to know them for a few months to a year before committing more fully. If the collaboration isn't going as expected, you can more easily end the agreement. Of course, that works both ways, which you could consider a downside—but I'd rather know early if the other person is itching to move on to something else. Keep in mind that the state and federal governments have regulations around whether an individual should be classified as a consultant or an employee—a topic worth discussing with your corporate attorney.

Let's talk through the steps that you'll be going through when you're looking to add employees or critical consultants to your team. I want to help you appreciate how the recruitment process should be adapted to meet the needs and resources of an early-stage scrappy startup. You won't have an HR department yet, but that doesn't make recruitment a less important function. At the same time, you are small enough to make quick decisions if things don't work out, so compared to a large company it will be easier for you to course-correct. Easier means faster here, as it will not be less painful from an emotional perspective.

We'll touch on five key aspects of the recruitment process: (a) scoping the role, (b) generating a candidate pool, (c) interviewing, (d) hiring, and (e) onboarding.

### Scoping the Role

In a small company setting, roles are not as strictly defined as they are in large companies. As a chief officer for palmm, there were days when I would pitch a VC in the morning, give our R&D engineer a hand testing electrical circuits over lunch, and then finish the day reviewing our market research! However, even if you want a new team member to be versatile, it remains important to think through what key projects they will have to accomplish and how the role may evolve from there. This will help drive the content of the job description for the role, as well as outline the skills you'll want to assess during the interview process. I found it particularly hard to do this for roles in which I had little or no personal experience. Accordingly, when I was looking for a new firmware engineer, I asked a previous colleague with experience in that domain to brainstorm with me. It is also helpful to review job descriptions of similar jobs on Indeed, Glassdoor, LinkedIn, and comparable websites to better understand what yours could look like. Relative to a large company's job description, the initial blurb about the company itself is much more important—this really needs to resonate with potential candidates. Look at Table 5.1 to see how I changed the company description for palmm, from a fairly specific description of our first indication and product focus, to a broader, more aspirational text.

When you are looking to hire, you have to decide if you need someone with a lot of experience or if you can get away with a less experienced individual. Needless to say, the latter approach will be more affordable, which every scrappy entrepreneur will consider a plus. I boil this decision down to two factors: (a) the importance of the job relative to the

*Table 5.1 Two versions of a company description to use in a job posting (reproduced with permission from palmm Co.)*

| From | To |
|---|---|
| palmm addresses a **dermatologic condition** that can have a dramatic impact on quality of life: excessive sweating, a.k.a. hyperhidrosis. This condition affects 15 million individuals in the United States alone. palmm solves unwanted sweat with an at-home once-a-week "electronic antiperspirant." Its **initial product** is an electrostimulation glove targeting excessive hand sweat. palmm is based at Fogarty Innovation, a top-notch medtech incubator that provides access to a wealth of experience and extensive network in the field. | palmm is a **medical technology company that leverages bioelectronics** to significantly improve people's quality of life. The company's initial focus is in dermatology. palmm was founded out of Stanford Biodesign and is located at Fogarty Innovation, a top-notch medtech incubator that provides access to a wealth of experience and extensive network in the field. palmm is **bringing together experts** in medical devices, consumer electronics, and industrial design to **develop noninvasive at-home therapies.** |

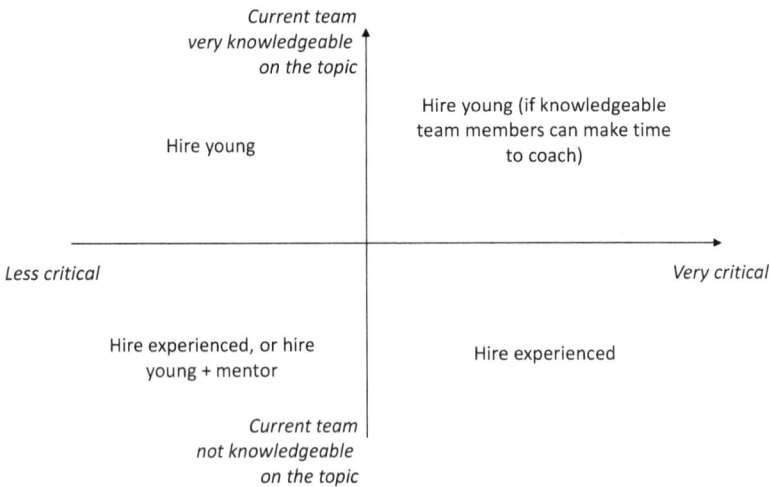

*Figure 5.1 Framework for deciding whether to hire young candidates or experienced ones*

project overall and (b) the current team's knowledge of that domain. Figure 5.1 illustrates this. If the topic is critical to the project and no one on the current team has that expertise (the bottom-right quadrant on Figure 5.1), you want to hire someone with a decent amount of experience. This is the quadrant I was in after my cofounder's departure when I needed someone to lead our R&D. If the knowledge does exist internally but there is not enough time to get the work done (the top-right quadrant), you can hire a less experienced individual—as long as the current team member(s) can make some time available to steer and coach. Over the years, I had a number of interns as part of my team who helped me on projects in this category, such as preparing market research studies (which I could easily coach on, given my past experience with McKinsey & Company) and conducting important but routine engineering tasks. If the topic is somewhat less critical, you can hire younger individuals more easily especially if the expertise exists within the team (the top-left quadrant). These are projects I would add to the intern's plate if I saw that they had additional bandwidth. If the expertise is not there yet (the bottom-left quadrant), consider whether you have a mentor or adviser who can help the younger individual be successful. At palmm, we failed to do this on the electrical engineering front. We knew we needed to develop a miniaturized, wearable power source for our device. It was not part of the critical path, as investors agreed with us that it was a feasible effort, it would just take time and money. After our initial plan with a connection of Justin's fell through, we had a junior engineer take over, but after a while we noticed the project wasn't progressing properly. Ultimately, we ended up hiring experienced electrical engineering consultants (hardware and firmware) for this later on, which led to much better results.

When you hire someone who is experienced, it is important to verify that they are still willing to roll up their sleeves. Experienced individuals may be used to outsourcing the actual work to more junior colleagues or to vendors. This behavior is not what you want at this stage of the company, as you won't have the people or funding to support it. You need capable people who can not only develop the strategy but also do the work every step of the way. Make sure to assess this during the hiring process to avoid making the wrong decision. This happened to me once, and it was painful to recognize this mistake too late. I'm still convinced the individual I had brought on was very capable. He just wasn't the right fit for us at that time. Telling him that he was let go was among the hardest moments in the lifetime of palmm for me, even though it was the right thing to do for the company.

The level of experience you need in a role should drive the title you attach to it. Many startups have a tendency to give early employees *chief officer* titles (CEO, CTO, COO, etc.). I think this is in part because we often start by needing to find investment, and investors want to see the highest-level folks in the organization. Putting the CTO in front of them will come across better than if they have to talk to an R&D Manager. My mentors advised against handing out these big titles in a blanket fashion, and I agree that it was forward-thinking of them. Essentially, if you start with these top roles, the only way to add more experienced individuals later will be to *downgrade* those who got the title in the first place, which is disappointing. There is also no way to give these early *chief officer* contributors a more formal promotion if they exceed expectations. So, rather than starting with the highest titles, my mentors recommended to start with *director* or *head of* roles if the person hadn't had higher titles in the past. You also don't want to under-title someone of course. For some, the title can be a bit of a negotiation, which is fine as long as it's not only a title they're after.

### Generating a Candidate Pool

Looking for suitable candidates for a job opening has similarities to looking for investor leads. It takes time to find the right person. As I mentioned at the start of this book part, I leveraged my network extensively and posted positions on LinkedIn Career and Indeed. I also sent connection requests and did cold outreach through LinkedIn Recruiter. You can use other platforms as well. For example, for an intern position, I reached out to a few universities and colleges nearby and was able to post on their internal platforms. If you have a company website, you can broadcast the job opening there, but it probably won't get seen unless you are able to drive traffic to your site.

When you're doing cold outreach (e.g., by sending an InMail message through LinkedIn Recruiter), your intro message should encourage the person to respond to you—even if it is just to say that they're not interested. On LinkedIn, where you pay for InMail messages, those that get any response (Reply or Not Interested) from a recipient within 90 days are credited back to the sender (Reed 2015), which discourages spamming. Here is a version of the message I used when I was looking for a head of R&D:

*Subject line: "Medtech startup looking to expand team"*
*Message:*

*"Dear [first name],*
*I am the CEO of palmm, a medical device startup that is developing a bio-electronics technology to improve people's quality of life. I am looking to expand our R&D team and came across your LinkedIn profile. Your experience with [enter something specific] is certainly relevant to our product. Would you be interested in having a chat?*

*I look forward to hearing from you.*
*Best regards,*
*Véronique"*

My hit rate was around 50 percent with this message. If your hit rate is much lower than that, consider tweaking the message, or narrowing your criteria for who you reach out to in the first place. Here is what I believe is key to success, also based on my own experience on the receiving end of similar outreaches:

- Address the recipient by their name. That's a first way of preventing your message from looking like spam.
- Introduce yourself and sign with your first name so that you come across as an approachable person.
- Pay extra attention to your word choice in the subject line and the first sentence, as these sections have the highest chances of being read.
- Describe the startup or project succinctly.
- Briefly explain why you think the recipient would be a good fit for the job opening. Referencing a particular position they had in the past will make it clear that you did some research before reaching out. You also want to make the recipient feel somewhat proud that their profile stood out!

- Include a question somewhere in the message, so that the recipient understands they're being asked to respond.
- Keep your message short, yet meaningful. You don't need to be too specific yet about the job opening, just signal that there is opportunity. I'd avoid including a link to a job posting if your goal is to have a conversation. If the person clicks on the link and becomes less interested because of the specifics, it's less likely that they will get back to you.

If you receive a positive response, you should suggest an informal phone conversation to get to know one another. And if that goes well, you can ask them to participate in the more formal interview process. Even if I didn't end up hiring anyone through this route, there was an individual who ended up reaching back out to me a year or so after we connected this way. He would have been a great candidate, but I'd already filled the position by that time.

Also, if the initial response is negative, do not hesitate to mention that they should feel free to share this opportunity with someone else who they believe may be a good fit.

Ask everyone who you want to invite for interviews for a resume before you interview them. You want to make sure you have a basic understanding of the person's past experience beyond what you can find on LinkedIn. If you get someone's name through a common connection, it's tempting to skip this step. However, asking for a resume confirms that you are taking the process seriously. If you want to meet the person informally first, you can. But once you decide that that person should be considered for the role you're looking to fill, you should request a resume before inviting them for a more formal interview.

In an ideal world, you generate a pool of three or more candidates first and then interview everyone around the same time. In practice, you may find that suitable candidates trickle in one by one, and decide to have people go through interviews as they come in. That's how I did it, as I preferred speed over perfect comparison. To increase diversity, aim to have more than one diverse individual in your candidate pool. According to research from *Harvard Business Review*, if there is only one minority individual in your candidate pool, there is statistically no chance that that person will be hired. The results change drastically when you have two or more minority candidates in your pool (Johnson et al., 2016). This may be hard for small startups in particular, as it may take you longer to source a sufficiently large and diverse pool, but I recommend keeping this in mind as an aspiration.

Given the similarities between finding investor leads and developing a talent pool, I ended up using an HR tracker that looks somewhat similar to my investor tracker. You can find my HR tracker template in the Scrappy Entrepreneur's toolkit (see page 103 for details on how to access this toolkit).

### Interviewing

I have been an interviewer in various settings: to hire new business analysts as a management consultant for McKinsey & Company, to help fill manager and director roles with Genentech, Inc., and to select fellows for Stanford University's prestigious Biodesign Innovation Fellowship. Each of these has rigorous interview processes to help ensure they select the best person for the job. For the first hires at palmm, I didn't think such a rigorous process was needed—we didn't even have enough people as part of our team to be able to put together a proper interviewer panel. However, over time, I learned that this is an area in which you do not want to take too many shortcuts. It just takes too much time and emotional toll if you get it wrong. And you will inevitably get it wrong at times, regardless of how rigorous your process is, so it's better to minimize those events as best as you can.

While I wouldn't directly copy any of the interview processes from larger institutions for the startup setting, I'll share the aspects that I do recommend incorporating in your interviews:

- While the main goal of the interviews is for you to assess the candidates, you should also give them a chance to *learn about your company and the team*. I like leveraging fundraising materials for this purpose. You will ultimately need to convince your top candidate that your company is worth them quitting what they are currently doing, so it's helpful for all candidates to learn about those things as they go through the interview process. That will also enable them to better tailor their answers to your questions.

- Ask questions to gauge the candidate's skills based on past experiences. These *Tell me about a time when…* questions allow the candidate to share past experiences that are relevant to the job opening. Their responses will give you a sense of whether the person could tackle the types of issues that will need to be addressed in the role you're hiring for. You should aim to ask all candidates the exact same questions in order to maximize fairness and objectivity. We inherently have biases when we meet new people. These biases may change the questions we ask and, consequently, change the way in which the candidate may respond to the question. If you present the same questions in the same order to each candidate, you help provide equal opportunities and can more easily compare apples-to-apples. Of course, in a startup, the job content may be somewhat flexible based on how the needs evolve and what the team member is capable of. With that in mind, you may need to vary the final questions a bit based on what you believe they may be able to do.

- Incorporate a *case study* in your interviews. I have found it helpful to rephrase the key issue I was dealing with in a way that would be understandable for an outsider (and without sharing confidential details) and have the candidate brainstorm solutions or solution approaches. If you're hiring for an R&D position, you can even make it a practical exercise. This portion of the interview is often the most revealing. It will really help you understand if the person is able to think on their feet and give you a sense of what they'll be able to accomplish on the job.

- Leave at least 10 minutes at the end of each conversation for *Q&A*. While Q&A time is a chance for the candidate to learn if they would enjoy the team and job, the questions the individual asks also help you assess whether the person understands the job, whether they have the right attitude for the startup world and the role, and how interested they are in the job overall. If their questions are overly generic in nature, that is generally not a good sign.

If you have other team members who can interview the candidate, take advantage of those *different perspectives*. If you do not have a direct team member who can act as an interviewer, have a trusted mentor or adviser do this for the top one or two candidates. This could be the *second-round* interview. If it would help you to share some more confidential details when testing the candidate's knowledge (e.g., for an R&D role), you could have the final one or two candidates sign a Nondisclosure Agreement (NDA) and talk in more detail after this. Keep in mind that an NDA is only worth as much as you trust the person. You will probably not be able to sue anyone in the early stage you're at anyway as that would be a costly endeavor in both time and money.

Finally, do not underestimate the value of *reference checks*. Make sure to talk to at least two individuals who recently worked with your top candidate. For one of my hires, I did talk with references, but their collaboration dated back about a decade. This is the person for whom I failed to identify that they were no longer able to roll up their sleeves the way my company needed them to, and I had to end this person's contract early.

When you're close to hiring the individual, spend a minute or two browsing the person's name on the web to see if there may be other things that need to be uncovered. A startup I knew well identified too late that the person they had hired for their clinical background had had their medical license revoked by the Medical Board of California. Even though it had nothing to do with the focus area of the startup, it substantially hurt the company's ability to fundraise. Had the founder done more research on the individual upfront, he would have been able to identify this early and discuss or address it before the person was hired.

## Hiring

Once you have found your top candidate, you're ready to make them an offer. When you are cash-constrained, coming up with a compelling offer may be a daunting task. The way I determine a fair compensation starts by estimating what this individual would get paid elsewhere. You can leverage your network to get comps, and there are vendors who either sell this type of info (e.g., Thelander) or who provide it at no cost in exchange for sharing your own stats (e.g., Glassdoor). The Bureau of

Labor Statistics also publishes wage data by occupation (Bureau of Labor Statistics, n.d.), even though those numbers always appear on the low end to me. Once you have a sense of a competitive total compensation (which may also include health care insurance, 401(k) benefits, and other perks with big companies), you can offer somewhat less cash and a bit more equity. Assume, for example, that the comps lead you to believe that $170,000 would be a competitive annual pay for an R&D Manager in the San Francisco Bay Area, plus a $10,000 bonus and the equivalent of $20,000 in stock options vested over 4 years. In that case, I might offer $165,000 cash, no bonus, and $100,000 in stock options (the latter vested over 4 years with a 1-year cliff). The total is a bit higher than the comp, but a bigger portion of it is compensated through riskier equity. How many shares the $100,000 equate to depends on your company valuation, which you should have a sense of from your fundraising efforts. I would not offer up this calculation to the candidate proactively but would explain the logic I applied if asked.

For part-time individuals, you could structure this as an hourly rate (assuming 8-hour workdays) or a monthly retainer, stating that you expect the person will work, for example, between 4 and 6 hours each month. Stating a range will make the agreement feel less transactional and will help ensure your contractor focuses on getting the work done rather than on the exact numbers of hours worked. You can also come up with more creative terms in the agreement, such as a milestone bonus. Have a corporate lawyer put the language together for you, as the devil is in the details, and the contract should include a set of standard clauses (e.g., assignment of inventions, confidentiality, etc.).

When you're hiring and cash-constrained, always think through whether there are others who may benefit from having you work with the person you're looking to take on board. For example, when I was looking for R&D interns, I got in touch with a professor at a local university who was in search of internship opportunities for his students. We were able to arrange a collaboration that enabled multiple students to benefit and contribute in various ways to the progress at palmm. I enjoyed working with each and every one of them!

Another creative structure I explored was to hire an individual jointly with two other startups. We offered our top candidate a full-time job, just split between three companies and paid by these companies together. The three CEOs agreed that this employee could move on to support just one of the companies once one of us was able to raise sufficient funds to sustain the employee full-time. Our candidate ended up not choosing the job, but I am still convinced that this strategy could have worked well for all of us.

Another possibility may be that your incubator has entrepreneurs-in-residence who can be shared resources among multiple companies at the incubator. In summary, don't be afraid to think out of the box when it comes to finding resources to get work done.

### Onboarding

In big companies, onboarding can be quite an ordeal, including several sessions and documents to get new hires up to speed on company jargon, organizational structure, compliance trainings, processes, and so on. With Genentech, I co-created an entire spreadsheet to help new joiners find what they might need in those first weeks and months. As a small company you won't need much in terms of onboarding materials, but you can still be thoughtful about what can make new team members feel welcome—a small welcome party, a lunch together, a tour of the facilities, a walk-through of your company documentation and processes. These are all inexpensive ways to help new hires get familiar with the rest of the team and what is available to them. As part of onboarding, you can discuss how you plan to track progress and set up a way of checking in with each other at a regular cadence.

---

### From Another Perspective: How to Make the Most Progress on a Tight Budget, Supported by Structured Hiring

The approach I took with palmm, in keeping the core team small and being extremely resourceful with funds, is one that I've seen others take as well. Eric Chehab, cofounder and CEO of Novonate, was able to develop a new medical technology for babies in intensive care, register the product with the FDA, launch it onto the market, and get his company acquired—with a team that was never larger than three W-2 employees. Quite a feat! Here is what he told me about his approach:

> I knew from the get-go that the market opportunity for our first product was real and important, yet small at around $20 to 30 million in the United States. Consequently, we had to limit how much money we raised from investors and remain lean to make it worthwhile for a future acquirer. Hiring the right people—those who are not just working to complete tasks, but are passionate about the field and hungry to get things done— was key to our success. Our product is not very complex, so we could get away with hiring early-in-career engineers and supplement our core team with consultants. That said, except for interns—of which we had many over the years—I always looked for individuals with some industry experience so that they would at least speak the language (e.g., understand what a quality system is). An eagerness to learn together and excitement to grow a company are what set our team apart. In terms of compensation, we did try to pay close to market rate, even though in part through stock options. In fact, I was the lowest paid person in the company for quite a while… To conserve cash, we worked out some interesting partnerships. For example, when we launched our product, we had a pretty much fully royalty-based payment model with our sales partner.

Eric's journey shows that the scrappy model can be successful, culminating in the acquisition of Novonate by Laborie in 2023. As of this writing, their device has been used on over 3,000 NICU (neonatal intensive care unit) babies and counting.

Anand Parikh, cofounder and CEO of diagnostics startup Chronus Health, has been very methodical about hiring:

> When we got going, our focus was on proving that the science worked, so we needed an R&D team. We hired entry-level

engineers as interns for a few months before offering them full-time jobs. This gave both us and them time to determine if the fit was right. Incorporating end-of-year bonuses in the compensation package was another way to keep costs low in the short term.

With regard to hiring, Anand indicated:

I'm a big fan of Patrick Lencioni, author of *The Five Dysfunctions of a Team* (Lencioni 2002) and other books on business management. His motto is to hire 'humble, hungry and smart'. Our structured hiring process is critical in assessing these aspects. It consists of four steps: a phone screen to assess basic communication skills, an online aptitude test, a technical conversation to gauge knowledge level, and an on-site demo. During the initial phone screen, we ask the candidates to talk about their background: If someone can't communicate about something they know better than us, it's not going to work. We have leveraged a pre-employment aptitude test called CCAT (Criteria Cognitive Aptitude Test) from the get-go and instituted a companywide threshold cutoff. Looking back at this data, we see a striking correlation between that score and high performance on the job. The technical conversation helps us gauge how knowledgeable the candidates truly are. Prior to the hiring decision we also make sure to get the candidate into the office. We show them our product and pay particular attention to the questions they ask. This gives us a sense of how hungry the candidate is to learn and deliver.

Reflecting on what he would have done differently, Anand indicates:

My cofounder Ashish and I forwent salary for quite a while. In hindsight, we should have taken one, even if just a minimal amount. Not getting a W-2 had some unexpected consequences. For example, it made getting a mortgage to buy a house much trickier for me.

The platform Chronus Health is working on is still in development, but Anand is optimistic. "We have already shown that the science and technology work, which is the holy grail in the blood diagnostics space."

## 2. Mentors and Advisers

Justin and I bounced our initial ideas off a couple of individuals from the get-go. They helped us think differently about our plans and identify blind spots, as good mentors do. Mentors can have different levels of engagement. There is no formal agreement specifying how they can or should support you. They are people with experience in a relevant field who are willing to donate their time to help you make progress and build leadership skills.

When we got going with the idea behind palmm, we initially involved three mentors. One of them, a professional investor, had been coaching startup teams for years. We would show her half-baked pitch decks, and she would help us understand how the story could be changed to be more impactful. She would also introduce us to people she thought might be interested in our work or have relevant skillsets for us. We got similar types of support from the successful CEO of a publicly traded medtech company and from a prominent serial medtech inventor and entrepreneur. When we joined Fogarty Innovation, our lead mentor helped us accelerate progress on the R&D front. Thanks to her, we started weekly *R&D sprints* that sped up our progress significantly. The goal became to show up to our weekly meetings with a new prototype, a good one or a terrible one—but at least something new that we had tried and learnt from. I also personally benefited (and still benefit!) greatly from working with the incubator's resident leadership coach. Particularly after my co-founder's exit, she became a much-needed sounding board, helping me ensure that I had evaluated a situation from different angles before determining the best path forward. These mentors and many, many more really helped guide our progress, and all of them did this either pro bono or because of our presence at Fogarty Innovation.

As I was so grateful for the contributions of our mentors and knew that they were truly improving our work at palmm, I initially included these individuals on our *team slide* for investor pitches. However, after a while I noticed that listeners didn't seem to appreciate the real value those mentors brought. There is no standard amount or type of support that mentors offer, so most investors will assume that these are simply figure-heads. Instead, they wanted to know about our *advisers*—individuals with expertise in a specific domain relevant to the business whose relationship with the company is determined through a formal agreement. We didn't have any of those, as in our experience we had gotten sufficient advice from the array of mentors we had the privilege of relying on.

While I still think mentors provide tremendous value, I do agree with investors that appointing a select number of relevant advisers can be powerful, as long as you choose them wisely. The adviser needs to have highly relevant expertise to be a long-term contributor to the company. The fact that there is a written agreement will tie the adviser's name to the company. This should make the adviser more driven to provide well-thought-out, long-term advice (even if a well-chosen mentor will do the same). This will give investors the confidence that you have this expertise on board, adding to the credibility of the company. Appointing an adviser should also open up your network to include theirs. Table 5.2 provides a more comprehensive list of differences between mentors and advisers.

Once I appreciated the distinction between a mentor and an adviser, I realized that we couldn't just continue to rely on mentors for advice on topics that potential investors saw as key risks for the company. In particular, we needed someone who could help signal to investors that

**Table 5.2 *Differences between a mentor and an adviser***

|  | Mentor | Adviser |
|---|---|---|
| *Documentation of commitment* | None | Formal agreement |
| *Level of support* | Highly variable | Determined through the agreement, e.g., 1–2 hours per week |
| *Compensation* | None | Typically equity-based compensation |
| *Type of support* | Often across multiple domains | Typically limited to a specific area of expertise |
| *Number* | As many as you like | Typically not more than 3–5 |

we were forward-thinking about our commercialization approach. I also thought that such an individual could eventually become a good independent board member.

I identified a number of individuals who I thought could make worthy advisers and then asked for mentoring help from them. Similar to the consult-to-hire strategy, it makes sense to have potential advisers be mentors for at least a few months before asking them to formalize the relationship. One individual I had considered to be a good adviser candidate would never connect me with his contacts. When I asked why not, he said that he was not comfortable doing so, as he was still fundraising for the company that he was running. That set alarm bells ringing for me: If this individual felt there was a conflict of interest, he was not to be the right person to be our adviser.

As mentioned in Table 5.2, advisers typically receive some type of equity-based compensation in exchange for their time and effort. When I was ready to appoint our first adviser, I went through a pretty extensive benchmarking exercise on this topic (thank you, StartX network!). For our pre-series A stage, I ended up settling on 0.25 percent in stock options vested over 3 years in return for 1 to 2 hours of service to the company per week. The vesting timeline is typically a bit shorter than for employees (3 and 4 years for palmm's advisers and employees, respectively). We did not include a cliff clause, as this is less common for advisers than employees (given the lower amount of options).

## 3. Vendors

It is an empowering feeling when you can put your first vendor to work. You give them instructions, then sit back and receive the detailed answers, results, or products! As the customer, you are the one getting pampered, a refreshing feeling coming out of fundraising efforts. The first vendor Justin and I worked with (beyond individual consultants) was Qualtrics, a survey platform that could also recruit survey participants. It was a very small engagement but valuable and rewarding nonetheless.

The search for the right vendor to do the work for you may take some effort, as any scrappy entrepreneur will be looking to be cost-effective once again. My goal is always to get at least two, and ideally three, competing quotes to choose from. Entrepreneur networks are incredibly helpful for sourcing initial recommendations. Trade shows such as Medical Device & Manufacturing (MD&M) and MEDevice (both with a focus on med-tech) are worth attending to find specialized vendors.

It has always been surprising to me how many vendors want to work with startups and overpromise on what they can accomplish. If you participate in pitch competitions, you will get connected with a whole lot of vendors who won't be the right fit for you but still want to spend time getting to know you and selling their business to you. And as your startup will be registered with various organizations, you'll start getting a cascade of e-mails from random vendors claiming that they are perfect for you. I recommend always starting the vendor search from a need you have, rather than the other way round. When various vendors introduce themselves to you, take their card and get a very high-level understanding of what they do, so that when you're in need of that type of vendor you can consider them in your pool. At that time, you can write a request for proposal and send it out to those you think could help.

Take your time on the quoting process. You want to get a clear idea of envisioned timelines and what happens if deadlines are not met. Don't pay everything upfront and, if you can, bake some milestone-based payments into the contract. You want to steer away from hourly or monthly fees where possible. I know several startups that outsourced portions of their technology development work, only to have to take it back months later after a lot of money spent.

You can be upfront about your cash situation (without giving exact details) and can ask for a price range early on in the process to avoid hours of back-and-forth before realizing that a vendor's price point is a magnitude above what you can afford. One way to do this is to ask whether they expect this work to be in the thousands, tens of thousands, or hundreds of thousands range. I have been surprised both ways with the answers I received to this question. Oftentimes the answer would be "oh, it's not that much, I expect about $150,000 to $250,000." In those cases, my heart would drop, as we didn't even have that amount of money in our bank account. I could quickly say that we were not ready to pay such amounts and that we could reconnect at a later stage, without the process drawing on. In one particular case, the answer ended up much lower than

I expected. I tried not to show too much excitement, but the internal relief was enormous given this was a vendor with tremendous expertise in a field we knew would be critical to our success. We ended up building a great relationship with this vendor.

Consider keeping some of your vendor relationships confidential. In general, I am not an advocate for remaining in *stealth mode*. The vast majority of startups benefit much more from sharing their story to help attract interest (without sharing proprietary details of course). The one exception I would consider is information about key vendor relationships. For complex R&D (or other) tasks it can be really hard to find the right vendor. Giving a competitor that information on a silver plate will ensure they have a much easier time making a similar product. By adding a clause in the NDA, you can ask the vendor not to disclose that they are interacting with you. In such cases, you should also avoid connecting with them on LinkedIn or engaging with them openly at public events such as at supplier conferences.

One final note on adding vendors to your team: Generally, you want to grow your team to (1) acquire skills you currently do not have and/or (2) get work done faster. However, I occasionally found myself looking to add to the team to fix something else: perception issues. When you're a founder, outsiders will naturally assume that you're biased toward positive outcomes. Having an external individual or company involved puts their reputation on the line with the results, which increases believability.

With palmm, we ran into this situation with our market research. I had done this type of work multiple times in my previous job as a management consultant, and large multinationals would pay a lot for the output. However, when we were about to kick off a new market research study, mentors recommended that we bring in a marketing consultant. Of course, it never hurts to discuss your approach and results with someone else who is knowledgeable on the topic, but, had it not been for those perception issues, we would have spent the money differently.

## 4. Your Network

A large relevant network is an invaluable asset for a scrappy entrepreneur. You will be tapping into it for many questions that you don't have immediate answers to. For palmm, we had the staff and fellow companies-in-residence at Fogarty Innovation, Stanford Biodesign alumni, and peers from MedTech Innovator, StartX, VentureWell E-Teams, and Stanford Venture Studio. Most of these groups have a mailing distribution list, Slack group, app, or other type of platform for Q&A purposes. These are very powerful as they allow you to ask any type of question related to your startup, from "How much should I compensate this type of adviser?" to "Can you please complete a quick survey about X?" and "Who can give me an intro to person Y?" I've generally gotten a decent set of responses within a day or two, and also learned from questions asked by others. This is a must for any entrepreneur: Make a conscious, proactive effort to expand and deepen your network over time.

# CHAPTER 6

# Unanticipated Team Changes

While growing your team can be stressful at times, it is mostly a happy process. Unanticipated departures, on the other hand, are not a fun experience. Whether it's because you didn't see it coming, it's hard to make the decision to let someone go, or you're having a hard time delivering the message, you'll need to keep your cool in these situations. Just remember—you're not the first one going through this, as my earlier examples with the departures of two colleagues testify. Unanticipated team changes can happen for three reasons:

- A team member decides to leave.
- You have to let someone go because they are not performing as expected or other unexpected reasons related to the individual.
- The team has to downsize because of cash flow issues.

I will share some considerations for each of these scenarios.

## 1. Voluntary Leave

While it may be sad to see someone go, you can accept it as an opportunity to reevaluate the needs of the business. That is what I did when my cofounder left. It was a chance to ask myself whether the company needed the exact expertise that he had brought to the team or if we would benefit from a different approach. For palmm at that time, I realized that it would be most helpful to have someone focused only on product development, and the person I brought on was able to fill that gap.

When someone leaves earlier than expected, you should also take a moment to review the cap table. If an early team member steps out, they take any stock that has vested with them. Unvested stock disappears unless it gets repurchased or reissued by the company. It makes sense to evaluate that situation. Potential investors get concerned by large amounts of dead equity[5], as that leaves less stock to incentivize future contributors.

When Justin left, we had been working on our project for roughly 2 years, so he was going to receive about half of the stock that he was allocated (given our 4-year vesting schedule). However, when we started our company, we had envisioned that we would be (surprise, surprise) much further along with our product than we were 2 years in. I advocated for reviewing our stock allocations as the road to success was most likely going to take longer. Justin did not agree with me on this: The contract said that he would receive a certain amount, so from his perspective it was only fair that that was what he should receive. The situation resulted in a number of heated discussions. Of course, I could understand where he was coming from. A contract is a binding agreement. Additionally, we started the company because of his initial idea that his condition could be an unmet need for others, and his contributions had been critical in coming up with our product approach. On the other hand, if I did not continue with the project, our equity would be worth zero dollars. Starting from that baseline, anything higher would represent a win. If we needed to readjust our stock allocations to get a better shot at ultimately helping patients by making more equity available to future contributors and decreasing investor concerns, I wanted to take that path. We agreed that it would be wise to have an objective third party sit in on our conversations. A mentor from our incubator, who we both trusted, agreed to take that role. While the conversations were still heated, this mentor helped us structure them better and resolve the situation more quickly and elegantly.

Through my network, I found a handful of other entrepreneurs who had experienced similar situations, and it was insightful to hear their perspectives on how to best go about this.

While these were tough conversations and we definitely needed some cool-off time afterwards, I'm happy to tell you that Justin and I were able to weather this storm. We even got to celebrate Thanksgiving and other events together again after the COVID-19 pandemic!

And if you're curious to know where we ended up, the answer is somewhere in the middle. Instead of retaining 46 percent of the shares he was initially allocated in the vesting schedule, Justin retained about 30 percent and the company repurchased the remainder. Even though *Never Split the Difference* (Voss and Raz 2016) is one of my favorite business books, the decision made sense and helped keep things moving forward.

## 2. Firing

If ever you realize that you have made a wrong hiring decision, act as soon as you have made that determination. After all, in a scrappy startup more than anywhere else, time is money.

To be able to realize that you have made a wrong hiring decision, you need to have a clear understanding of what *good* looks like even before a new hire gets started. Over the first weeks and months, you can then compare the reality against that envisioned ideal. Have regular check-ins with your team, so that you can give them feedback. If they are under-performing or otherwise not contributing as desired, that will give them a chance to course-correct. I like doing this during a short walk or over a coffee, as that feels less formal than a sit-down in a conference room.

If you decide that you have to fire an individual, make sure to practice the delivery of that message. While in a large company your HR partner can step in, in a small startup this difficult task lands on your shoulders. A personal coach or a trusted mentor can help you prepare. For example, my coach noticed that I was overly focused on apologizing when delivering the hard message. It's much better to remain factual, state that you have come to a decision, and provide a brief rationale for that decision. Apologizing is not going to make anyone feel better.

When you fire someone, make sure you take care of other team members during this time. They may have questions when they see a colleague depart, so make sure you have answers ready for them.

## 3. Layoffs

Unfortunately, I also had to live through this third *unanticipated-team-change* scenario: laying people off (or ending consulting agreements).

There came a time with palmm when we got very low on cash. My first action was to minimize our outside spend. This means either deciding not to kick off certain projects or doing some work internally instead of outsourcing it. With palmm, I decided not to start a firmware engineering project as it was not on the critical path to de-risk product development. I also had an intern prepare documents for our quality system and reviewed them myself, instead of working with a more expensive consultant. However, you cannot just switch off salaries and consulting retainers. So, at some point, you will have to tell people they are being let go. From a personal perspective, you would like to give contributors a heads-up that they may need to start looking for a new job. However, from the company's perspective, you want to avoid having good people leave the company early. There is no single right answer for a tiny startup as to when is the best time to tell contributors that the bank account is approaching zero. I had a detailed model of our spending and different scenarios of how far we could stretch it, and, based on that, I determined that we would be able to stay alive until July 2020, assuming no money came in by then. I chose to start telling people about the precariousness of the situation in April. I continued to show optimism about our chances of completing a funding round before July but indicated that we would be out of money by that time if we were unsuccessful. My contributors were all part-time, so I figured that the chances of them walking away were lower than for full-time employees as they could always continue to moonlight. Also, the COVID-19 pandemic had only just begun, so I figured it was going to take them some time to find new engagements since many companies were in a holding pattern for hiring at that time. This heads-up was appreciated by all.

# CHAPTER 7

# Communicating About the Team

A strong team is obviously going to help you get a lot done, but it also instills confidence in potential investors about your ability to be successful. What you say, and don't say, about your team can truly make or break a deal, so you want to be well prepared for investor conversations on this front. As mentioned in the *Pitch Deck* section on page 34, info on your team is one of the top five topics to include in any pitch deck. When a potential investor looks at pitches, they generally assume that you are overstating things. For a team slide, that could mean the following:

- When you mention who is part of your team, they may assume this is a side gig for everyone.
- If you call out a mentor, they might assume that this individual isn't very involved at all.
- If you don't list credentials, they'll assume the worst.

Let me share two examples of *team slides* that I used for palmm and highlight key elements to consider as you build versions for your company.

To be clear, I don't think the team slides from Figures 7.1 and 7.2 are perfect. I just want you to appreciate how we thought through this at different stages of the company.

We created the team slide from Figure 7.1 within a half year of coming up with our unmet need and solution concept, prior to incorporating the company. As you can tell, we didn't really have much of a team yet—and that is something that you cannot work around. As we didn't have a company yet, we didn't have official titles and, instead, called ourselves *technical* and *business* cofounders. It helped quickly indicate what each of us contributed.

### The team

**Justin Huelman,** Technical co-founder
- Has the condition
- MS Biomedical Engineering
- 5 years medtech R&D experience
- '15-'16 Stanford Biodesign Fellow

**Véronique Peiffer,** Business co-founder
- PhD Mechanical Engineering
- Engagement manager (McKinsey & Company)
- '15-'16 Stanford Biodesign Fellow

**Strong mentor network**       STANFORD BYERS CENTER FOR
BI◯DESIGN

- Uday N. Kumar, MD, founder iRhythm and Element Science *(wearable medtech)*
- Sean Mehra, Head of Product HealthTap *(consumer health tech)*
- Renee Ryan, VP Venture Investments Johnson & Johnson *(VC)*

palmm

*Figure 7.1 palmm's pre-company team slide (slightly adapted with permission from palmm Co.)*

Overall, the slide is relatively text-heavy. Using logos could have helped make this easier to read,[10] as people rarely read through text during a live presentation.

Seeing this slide myself years after having created it, the phrase "Strong mentor network" feels a bit contrived. Our intent was to signal that we were well supported, highlighting three mentors who were able to lend expertise on key aspects of our venture: wearable medtech, consumer health, and fundraising. Highlighting advisers would have been better, but we didn't have advisers at the time—and, of course, you shouldn't rush appointing advisers simply because you want to be able to call them out on a team slide. It's far more important to take your time and select the right individuals. Also note that calling out an investor as a mentor when their fund has not invested in the company is suboptimal because the question will always be: Why haven't they invested?

Finally, keep your audience in mind when you design this slide. The version of Figure 7.1 might work great for a presentation related to a grant application. An investor pitch slide, on the other hand, may benefit from more defined founder job titles and omission of the words "Strong mentor network," combined with a convincing voiceover on how these individuals will continue to support you.

The slides shown in Figure 7.2 come from a deck when I was pitching for a $15 million series A round. It was a larger deck, so I could get away

**palmm has leveraged top-notch expertise to develop its core technology**

**Founding team**

BIODESIGN

**Véronique Peiffer**, PhD, Full-time CEO
• Stanford Biodesign alum
• PhD Mechanical Engineering
• Former Manager McKinsey & Co

**Justin Huelman**, MS, Technical advisor
• Stanford Biodesign alum
• MS Northwestern University
• Livongo Labs Lead

**Daniel Francis**, MS
*Mechanical engineering*
Former VP of R&D at Miramar
Labs (hyperhidrosis technology)

**Preston Brown**, BS
*Electrical engineering*
Vast experience in medtech and
consumer electronics

**Fiona Sander**, MS
*Project manager*
Experienced medtech
consultant

**Lana Widman**, MS
*Quality engineering*
Credentialed Auditor for
ISO and EU regulations

**Kei Castleberry**
*Junior engineer*

palmm    After closing of the Series A financing, palmm will transition to a 3-4 FTE full-time team

**The team is supported by expert collaborators and advisors in dermatology and medtech more generally**

**Dan Siegel**, MD
*Dermatologist*
Former President American
Academy of Dermatology

**Marlyanne Pol-Rodriguez**, MD
*Dermatologist (Stanford
Medicine)*
PI on previous clinical study

**Pat Altavilla**
*30+ years M&S
dermatology/aesthetics*

**Incubator support**
Office space and support
of >250 years of combined
medtech expertise

**Matt Davidson**, PhD
*Founder and former CEO
Verrica Pharma (IPO 2018)*

**Dennis Brown**, PhD
*Drug discovery and
development
(dermatology, oncology)*

**Nancy Isaac**, JD
*Regulatory advisor*
Experienced startup
regulatory consultant

**Boutique IP firm**
Other clients include
The Foundry, Medtronic

**Peter Townshend**, JD
*Corporate legal*
Former partner with
Perkins Coie

palmm

*Figure 7.2  palmm's pre-series A team slides (slightly adapted with permission from palmm Co.)*

with using two full slides. The benefit of having two slides is that you can make a clearer distinction between *core team members* (first slide) and advisers and collaborators (second slide).

Most of the people on the first slide were part-time contributors, but I did not call that out explicitly. As investors generally assume the worst, I figured they would make that assumption anyways (which is why I added *full-time CEO* next to my own name to clarify that I was fully committed to this company). Some investor candidates will ask whether contributors will join full-time once you have sufficient money in the bank (assuming you could use their expertise in a full-time capacity). Ideally, you can say yes to that question so they know it will be easy for you to ramp up once funds are available. If you can't, think carefully through how you will fill that skill gap. As you can see, I had both cofounders on the slide even though Justin was no longer involved on a day-to-day basis. This was a conscious decision. Justin's name would be visible on the cap table, so I wanted to avoid a surprise later on. If questions came up, I was careful about how I explained why Justin was not an active contributor. As part of the conversations surrounding his departure, we had agreed on the language we would use to ensure that our recaps were in sync. Even the slightest difference could deter potential investors.

I was a lot more targeted with word choice on these slides, as compared to the pre-company version from Figure 7.1, with the goal of instilling confidence in the audience that we were covered across all aspects of this project.

Also note that the titles of these slides guide the reader's thinking more than the ones from the pre-company team slide. I did not call out vendors, but if you have any key ones that you think will add to the credibility of your story, you can include them (unless you decide to keep that information confidential).

Should a team slide come at the beginning or at the end of your presentation? Opinions differ on this front. My take, after trying out both ways and observing other companies' approaches during pitch competitions, is that you should only put your team slide at the beginning of your presentation if the team is a slam-dunk winning team. If that is the case, the audience will be so *wowed* by the team slide that they may be too intimidated to ask further questions! If your team does not (yet) fall into that category, I recommend keeping the team slide for the end. When you get on stage or sit down to start the conversation, you should briefly introduce the people present so that the listeners don't have to wonder who they're dealing with throughout the presentation. But keep the team details for the end once you have convinced them that you know what you're talking about.

In summary, it can be hard to show a well-rounded team, particularly in the early days where you really don't have one yet. But you want to have the audience feel confident that you are surrounded by talent and that you will be able to continue to build out your team along the way.

# CHAPTER 8

# Team Health

Leaders put their stamp on a team's health, and I would argue that holds even more true for a small startup given the leaders are a lot more visible to everyone. We'll talk about building team culture, being mindful of work–life balance, and what mindset a scrappy entrepreneurial journey takes. You'll also find two "From Another Perspective" inserts in this chapter, with contributions from three inspiring leaders.

## 1. Team Culture

While you can find many resources on the topic of team culture, one of my mentors, the serial medtech entrepreneur who heads up Fogarty Innovation, told me: "If you don't build a team culture, it will build itself." That rings true to me to this day. And that is why I don't want to skip the topic here.

When Justin and I started working on the idea behind palmm, we developed a mission statement for our project (Figure 8.1). With just the two of us, it was easy enough to agree on what should be in there. Here is what we created:

"Our mission is to become life-long contributors to the field of medical device innovation. We will do this by:

- Building a team we believe in
- Creating an experiential learning opportunity
- Being reflective of the process and skills to make it repeatable
- Engaging in our networks
- Enjoying being passionate about work."

Some elements of this statement are relevant for a project, but less so for a company. We didn't go to the extent of defining values, but that certainly would have been a good thing to do as well.

*Figure 8.1  palmm's cofounders in front of the project's mission statement (with permission from palmm Co.)*

I am a big fan of giving and receiving feedback, a practice that was ingrained in me during my management consulting years. At palmm, we set up monthly check-ins as cofounders to review how we were doing with our team culture. Justin observed that I had a tendency to talk over people when I got too excited, so I would work on waiting my turn. I would tell Justin that I didn't like starting important projects late in the afternoon, as it invariably delayed dinner time, and he would try to be more mindful of his timing. With a small team, it was fairly simple to understand what others liked and what frustrated them and adjust our working style accordingly.

As a team grows, however, it becomes harder to know what everyone wants and needs and what the core values are. To give you an example, we had one engineering consultant working for us who was excellent at her job but was always negative about other people's work. When she posed a question, it would invariably come across as an insult to others on the team. Initially, I thought that the other consultant she worked closely with was underperforming. But when I asked a friend to review the consultant's work, he told me that the output was top-notch. After a couple of months of dealing directly with the toxic consultant and giving her critical but constructive feedback, I decided to replace her. It was a hard decision as her work was great and now we needed to find someone else—but it really lifted my spirits to no longer have to deal with the negativity surrounding this individual. Had we been more proactive about defining our company values and sharing with the broader team, we may have been able to address this issue even earlier.

You can set expectations by crafting a mission statement and defining of core values and then making sure that those are understood. After that, it's important to practice what you preach and create an open environment. You want to make sure that people not only do their work but also feel like they can have other conversations. Especially if you have a team of part-timers, give them a chance to get to know each other, for example, by having people come together for a lunch or a happy hour.

As the leader, make sure to check in with everyone on a regular basis. They are devoting part of their professional career to this company and to you, so you want to help them make progress on their journey and enjoy it. If the company fails, they'll still reap the benefits of having worked in a fun and stimulating environment. It's an important and rewarding responsibility for any leader.

## 2. Work–Life Balance

When I started palmm, I didn't have a lot of personal obligations. I had moved to the United States a year prior and made some new friends, but, overall, I did not know that many people here. As I was in a long-distance relationship, I didn't even get to spend much time with my then-boyfriend (now-husband) who had stayed behind in Belgium. So, most of the time I was working. I did not have to be back home at a certain time, and

I didn't have to explain myself when going to bed late. It wasn't hard to focus. In a small startup like palmm, there is always more that you can do, and there are never sufficient hours in the day or week. Moreover, there is no one telling you what to do, so you have to decide for yourself what should be done next. This is liberating but also demanding. In a previous job as a management consultant, I had to *protect weekends* to stay sane. At my startup, that wasn't the case as the motivation to get more done was internal. Still, it gets harder and harder—as more stakeholders get involved, more obligations come your way—and you can't delegate much in a scrappy startup.

Even after I got married and my husband was able to move out here, he understood how important the success of this startup was to me and fully supported my long days in the office.

Still, I tried to have some balance between time at work and life outside of it. I don't like eating junk food, so sitting down to a proper dinner was always a way to unwind and reset. When I moved to the San Francisco Peninsula, I made a commitment to myself to do something new each week, whether it was going for a hike or baking bread with one of my housemates. With perfect weather and easy access to parks and trails, I was always willing to fit in a run. And I tried to find a piano to practice on when I could.

At palmm we never formalized vacation time, but startups with a higher number of salaried employees should make decisions on this topic to ensure clarity and consistency.

## From Another Perspective: How to Balance Early Startup Life with Family and Friends

I am always impressed when I talk with scrappy startup entrepreneurs who have a family to take care of. Not only do you need to be more careful about trade-offs between work and life outside of it, but the financial pressure and impact of uncertainty are magnified as well.

Iris Wedeking, cofounder and CEO of iDentical, has been doing this for 5 years with a husband who also works, and 3 children between the ages of 10 and 15, one of whom has special needs. She is lucky to have family close by, but it remains a careful balancing act between her work bringing a drill-free dental implant to the market and her family time. When I asked her about it, she explained:

> It is important to set boundaries. Initially, for me that meant not working during weekends. During the week I would work till 6 p.m., spend time with family, and then get back to my desk after the kids went to bed. I am definitely a bit of a workaholic, so when I got started again at night, I would generally continue till 1 or 2 a.m. However, through conversations with my personal mentor, I recently realized that it doesn't have to be that way. So, just a few months ago, I changed my routine. I now consider not working at night as the default, and only make exceptions to that rule when it's really needed. To my surprise, it has made everything less stressful, maybe because sleep certainly is important as well. I'm not sure if I'm more efficient during the day, but I do think I'm a bit better at prioritizing, instead of just assuming I will get more done during the night. Currently, fundraising is my number one priority. So, if anything else comes my way, I feel more comfortable about pushing some of that work to a future date.

Bronwyn—who you already heard from in the "From Another Perspective: Fundraising without Guilt" insert on page 49—is a pediatric cardiologist by training and mother of three. She had her third child while she was the CEO of Tueo Health. She added an interesting perspective:

> I had my first two children during medical residency and fellowship, respectively. That was physically challenging because of the long hours and not even sleeping in my own bed while on call. Having a newborn as the CEO of a tiny startup was more mentally challenging. I felt like I had to put on a happy face for everyone. As a doctor in training, my colleagues and even patients were very understanding of my situation. I was

> allowed to say that it was hard, and they would commiserate with me to some extent. While fundraising and even spending time with my colleagues as a CEO, however, I felt isolated and that made it extra hard for me. I went back to work when the baby was just two weeks old, but that wasn't all that bad as I could do it on my own terms and I loved my job.

## 3. The Entrepreneurial Mindset

The topic of mindset already came up with fundraising (see the *Fundraising Flair* section on page 48). In this section, we'll zoom out and discuss how the right mindset can help you through the entrepreneurial journey more generally.

A common thread running through this book is that the life of a scrappy entrepreneur is hard. The comparison with a roller coaster really is an appropriate one. One day, a success with a key experiment in the lab makes you feel on top of the world. The next day you feel like a loser because yet another investor turned you down. So how do you survive? What keeps entrepreneurs going? For me, it is a blend of keeping in mind the bigger goal and the excitement that comes with the inherent variety of the job. If I wasn't passionate about wanting to improve people's lives, I don't think I would have had the persistence needed to keep going. The passion and commitment to the cause is critical, since knowing that there is a bigger goal you want to achieve helps you get through the rough days. And, while always doing something different can be tiring, it is incredibly rewarding for someone like me who is always thirsty to keep learning and growing. To weather it all, you certainly need to have a good dose of grit and a can-do attitude.

I am an inherently impatient individual. I like to get answers fast and want to get moving. Being an entrepreneur taught me to be more *zen* about everything that is thrown at me. At Fogarty Innovation, I was introduced to the world of mindfulness, thanks to a course that our professional coach organized for the incubating companies. I can't claim to practice meditation consistently, but the philosophy has helped me stay calm in tricky situations and be more resilient overall. It's a skill that is useful both professionally and at home with two kids running around.

# From Another Perspective:
## Mindset

Let's go back to the two entrepreneurs, Bronwyn and Maria, who provided their perspectives on fundraising mindset (see page 49), to hear about challenges on their journeys and how they were able to persist.

Bronwyn agreed with me that the hardest part about being an entrepreneur is the day-to-day uncertainty.

> One day you're over the moon because you just got invited to a big meeting to present as one of three companies. But then, when it's over, you have both feet on the ground again, and maybe nothing came from that meeting even if you felt that it had gone exceptionally well. Uncertainty also prevails on the financial side. There were times where we, as founders, decided not to take a salary for a month, just so that we could pay our employees.

When I asked her what made her persevere, her answer was that she was truly committed to the need she was addressing.

Maria also talked to me about her mindset. She has had an unconventional path to entrepreneurship and her remarkable story could easily fill a book by itself. Maria said:

> Whenever things were hard, I would think back about where I came from. I had to be an adult at a very young age as my mother passed away when I was 13 and my dad left me behind with my two younger brothers. I went to work as a medical device assembler while going to a community college to get an engineering degree. No one would have invested in me as a person, and I still made it work. If I was able to get through that, I could do anything.

Maria points to early fundraising as the most difficult part of her first founder experience, as we discussed in the *From Another Perspective* section on page 49.

# CHAPTER 9

# Key Takeaways from Part 2—Team

## ☀ Key Learnings

1. Cofounders are those core team members in the early beginnings of the company who are willing to take the risk to stick around. Look for cofounders who are relentless and make you better as a team. Make sure you (get to) know them well enough before embarking on the journey together.

2. Cofounder compensation strategy: Do not hesitate to indicate to investors what you are really worth, but at the same you should also be prepared to not get paid this full amount from the beginning.

3. Set a vesting schedule for founder's stock. A 4-year clock with a 1-year cliff is typical (at least in the medtech industry) but consider upfront if this is really enough time to move the needle.

4. Make key contributors feel like they are truly part of your team, even if they are only working part-time for you and even if they are not employees. Find ways to convey the experience of being part of a bigger whole (e.g., by organizing a happy hour or other team event).

5. Adopt a *rent-before-you-buy* approach for hiring: When possible, have new team members consult with the company before you employ them and seek mentorship first from candidate advisers.

6. When hiring for a role you aren't an expert in yourself, get advice from mentors or friends with expertise in the domain.

7. Always consider whether you really need someone with a lot of experience or if the existing team has the know-how (and sufficient bandwidth) to coach a less experienced individual. This also depends on the importance of the job to the project overall.

8. Every team member of a scrappy startup needs to be excited about and capable of rolling up their sleeves.

9. Be careful with handing out big titles for less experienced team members. You can always promote, but it's hard to demote.

10. Be rigorous in your interviewing process. You want to avoid too many hiring mistakes. Being rigorous means obtaining a resume, properly structuring the interviews (potentially including aptitude tests), including a case study in the interview, having at least one other person interview the final one or two candidates, and calling up two or three references for them.

11. Always keep working on expanding your network. Among other advantages, it will help you create a larger and more diverse candidate pool for any vacancy when the need arises.

12. Be creative when hiring: Are there other entities (universities, other startups, incubators, etc.) that you can partner with?

13. Fair compensation can be determined by estimating what the new team member would get paid in a different job. Startups can get away with offering less cash and more equity.

14. Mentors can be fantastic resources; however, in the eyes of (potential) investors, advisers who support the company through a structured agreement carry more weight.

15. Before the official quoting process starts, ask whether a potential vendor expects the rough scope of work to be in the thousands, tens of thousands, or hundreds of thousands. This will help you avoid spending unnecessary time gauging prospective vendors that you cannot afford.

16. Consider keeping key vendor relationships confidential to preserve an edge over the competition.

17. Have an objective party sit in on team conversations that risk getting heated.

18. When you fire someone, practice delivering the message. You want to be factual and succinct.

19. If layoffs are imminent, decide how much advance notice is appropriate for your situation. Give too much notice, and you may see team members leave prematurely. Give too little notice, and you may lose the respect of your team.

20. The *team slide* is a critical portion of any pitch. Especially if your team is small, you want to think carefully about how a potential investor may interpret each word and visual on the slide. Think about balancing text and logos and highlighting credentials that need to jump out. Consider the trade-offs of including mentors.

21. If you don't build a team culture, it will build itself. Make shaping your team's culture a conscious effort.

22. Learn to set your own boundaries when it comes to work–life balance, as you will have no one else helping you make that happen.

## Key Tools and Resources Provided

- Discussion on how to approach founder equity allocation: https://startupguide.hbs.edu/people/founding-team/co-founder-equity-splits-ways-to-approach-allocations/
- HR tracker template: Included in the Scrappy Entrepreneur's toolkit
- Employment and wage estimates from the Bureau of Labor Statistics: www.bls.gov/oes/

Note: Visit veroniquepeiffer.com to receive a copy of the Scrappy Entrepreneur's toolkit.

# PART 3

# All the Small Stuff
# That Adds Up

What I hadn't imagined before starting palmm is how much time I'd have to spend on mundane tasks. Keeping accounting books up to date, ensuring vendor payments and tax documents get submitted on time, keeping track of investor conversations, making small changes to pitch decks, booking travel, getting liability insurance, staying on top of IP lineages in various countries—*all of this and more falls on you when you're a scrappy entrepreneur.* This list is just a sliver of all the small stuff that adds up to full days during which you don't really move the needle for your company. Most of these activities could be outsourced, but that costs money. And even if you opt to invest in software support, you're still ultimately responsible for the accuracy of the content. One day I noticed that our people management software had made a mistake in our filings. As a result, we had overpaid the state of California by $2,500—a big sum of money for a small company like ours. The software company told me that I could get the money back by getting in touch with the Employment Development Department (EDD) in California directly. I decided to pursue it, but it took me hours on the phone trying to get a hold of a customer service representative at the EDD and months to retrieve the money.

While there is no way to get around all that small stuff that adds up, I personally wish I had had a better idea of what to expect to avoid the many surprises I encountered during my entrepreneurial journey. Providing a sense of everything that will end up on your plate is the core objective of Chapter 10. Then, we'll dive into what you can do to lighten the burden. To start, the fellow entrepreneurs you met in previous chapters shared some handy best practices with me. Those tips, as well as my own, form the basis of Chapter 11. I promise that reading this entire section will help better prepare you for your role as a scrappy entrepreneur. While the content is a bit dense, the section is concise so that it will be easier to refer back to. And if you find a way to cost-effectively outsource it all, give a copy of the next three chapters to the person who will be doing this type of work for you!

# CHAPTER 10

# What Not to Forget About

Many of the activities that fall on the plate of the scrappy entrepreneur and are not part of the project's critical path are relatively simple tasks that may need to be done on a regular basis. It is the simplicity and/or recurring nature that make these tasks burdensome for entrepreneurs, as we typically prefer learning something new and exciting over mindless or repetitive tasks.

Based on my experience, these activities fall into eight buckets, which form the sections of this chapter. I'll start by telling you a bit more about the various registrations and reporting requirements that you need to work through as a scrappy entrepreneur. Next, I'll share my thoughts on how to manage (digital) documents and get your feet on the ground regarding who will be hauling around deliveries and dealing with other light manual work. I'll give you a sense of what to expect with vendor selection and recurring payments. We'll close out the chapter with managing your company's IP portfolio, its public image, and some final reflections.

## 1. Registrations and Applications

I remember that I felt some level of excitement about the first registrations that made it to my plate. Simple acts such as registering a web domain and creating a LinkedIn profile bearing our freshly minted, homemade company logo validated that we were *real*, even prior to the incorporation of the company.

Incorporation, in our case prompted by the need to accept a check on behalf of the company, officializes it all and is, in a way, a registration by itself. Our attorney handled the incorporation paperwork, as we did not want to get it wrong. I have seen other entrepreneurs do this independently, leveraging free online incorporation packages as you can find through www.CooleyGO.com, for example.

There are other legal registration requirements beyond the incorporation in the U.S. Companies need to register with the state they operate in,
possibly obtain licenses or permits from their county or city, apply for an
Employment Identification Number (EIN), and get an account with the
state's department of employment once they have employees. Many states
also require you to have a registered agent who can receive important com-
munications. If you do not have a physical (business) address in your state
of incorporation, you have to work with a vendor for this. I barely ever
received any communication through that route, but we still had to identify such a vendor (incserv in our case) and pay for the service every year.

The first time we applied for a government grant, it became clear to
me that funding-related applications could become burdensome. As part
of the SBIR application process, we needed to register with the System
for Awards Management (sam.gov), get a unique nine-digit identifier for
the business assigned by Dun & Bradstreet (a DUNS number) through
a different platform, register with yet another system called Fastlane, register as a Small Business Concern (SBC) by filling out another form, and
probably other steps that I have since forgotten. I don't want to anchor
you to these exact steps as they may change over time. (For example,
I learned that the need for a DUNS number has since been replaced with
the need for a Unique Entity ID.) The point is that it took us hours to
understand what exactly was needed, and multiple days to complete the
process, especially because for certain steps, we needed to wait for a con-
firmation or ID before we could move on to the next step. And all of this
before we had even started writing the grant application itself.

Applications to pitch with angel groups and for pitch competitions
are much less burdensome in that regard, but they do still often require
the completion of an online form. As you are not always able to save your
responses directly from those forms, I recommend copy-pasting your responses in a digital notebook. Not only will this help you complete future
applications, as most questions are similar in nature, it will also help you
remember what you shared with whom.

Holly (see the "From Another Perspective" insert on page 12) goes
one step further with documenting: Whenever she registers on a website
and believes that she will have to come back to it for a renewal or payment or so, she jots down the steps she had to work through in her digital

notebook, so that she can refer to it easily the following year. A great idea if you ask me!

There will be many other registrations and applications that you'll find yourself working through in addition to the examples I share here. With each of these requiring at least a username and a password, I highly recommend using a password management software (LastPass, iCloud, McAfee, Google Password Manager, etc.), or a simple list of mnemonics to help you remember them.

## 2. Required Reporting

Many of the agreements your company will get into come with an obligation to report certain data on a regular basis. Some reporting requirements are legal but noncontractual in nature, and others are contract-related. And sometimes you are expected or strongly encouraged by investors and other stakeholders to report back to them.

During my Biodesign Innovation Fellowship year at Stanford University, an entrepreneur advised us to postpone incorporation as long as possible. I only truly appreciated why he had made that recommendation a year or two after we incorporated. Before that time, we were operating as a project out of the university. We had grants to manage, so we already had some budget management to do. However, once we had incorporated, the number of recurring reporting requirements began to accumulate. It starts with having to submit tax returns at both federal and state levels. When you incorporate your business in one state but operate out of another, you have requirements in both of those states. Our company was incorporated in Delaware, but we were operating out of California, as is the case for many innovation-driven startups. The first year when we had to submit taxes, I did it myself, with just a bit of help from a friendly accountant through a phone call and a few e-mails. As we didn't have employees or sales income, it was a straightforward submission. While California has a minimum franchise tax of $800 (in 2024), we benefited from the exception that the state grants in the first taxable year. At the end of that first year, we also had to file an annual report in Delaware, which came with a $450 minimum annual franchise tax for us (and an absolute minimum of $175, plus a $25 to $50 flat fee, in 2024

[Delaware Division of Corporations 2019]). These tax amounts go up as your company's revenue increases. For the second year, our submission got a bit more complex, as we had employees on payroll and had opened a convertible note seed fundraising round. Afraid to do something wrong, I paid an accountant based in Kentucky to help us out. He came recommended by a fellow StartX entrepreneur. As we were low on cash, I asked him what I could do myself so that he would just have to verify my work. He got me started with Quickbooks to get our accounting in order, and we collaborated on the submissions for that year and the following ones. For tax returns, you can also leverage other types of software, such as TurboTax Business, which I have used more recently. These types of software may not automatically take advantage of less well-known laws, such as R&D tax credits, so it's best to check with someone who knows what to look out for. If you start doing things yourself, keep it organized so that it will be easy to hand over once you have that luxury.

Once you hire employees or consultants, you have to start managing payroll, which comes with quarterly and annual obligations (e.g., contribution returns and 1099-NECs). There are various software solutions to help you with this (e.g., Gusto, TriNet, and ADP).

These days, many official entities have useful websites that clearly detail all the steps that you need to follow to stay on track. I'll include a few of the most relevant websites here so that you can benefit from them. Keep in mind that these may change over time and that you will need different websites if you incorporate in and/or operate out of other states.

- Delaware Division of Corporations—https://corp.delaware.gov— where Delaware corporations file their annual report and pay business entity tax
- California Franchise Tax Board—www.ftb.ca.gov/file/business— with information on doing business in California
- California Secretary of State—https://bizfileonline.sos.ca.gov— where companies operating out of California need to file an annual or biennial Statement of Information
- State of California's Employment Development Department— https://eddservices.edd.ca.gov—which you'll need to register on once you have employees in California

The reporting obligations we have discussed so far are legal but non-contractual in nature. Other types of reporting may be necessary to comply with contracts you have signed. For example, our IP licensing agreement with Stanford University had annual requirements, as well as milestone-based reporting asks linked to FDA submission and revenue targets. These types of requirements can be particularly hard to stay on top of, as no one proactively reminds you of them. Using a *compliance calendar* can come in handy. For more on this tip, see page 123.

A different type of reporting relates to investors. Some investors request regular written reports so that they can update their backers on how their funds are being used. One impact fund on palmm's cap table requests yearly reports on progress toward improving people's lives. In the *From Another Perspective* section on page 12, Holly from Madorra also referred to this type of requirement with SBIR grants. One benefit of this that she highlighted is that the resulting report can be repurposed to help complete other written documents. Still, such requirements add deadlines to your calendar, and the amount of time you spend on them adds up. I therefore always do my best to right-size it. Some investors may ask for a document but file it away without even looking at it. Gauge what is needed and don't overdo it.

As we are on the topic of investor updates, even if they don't ask for them, it is good practice to keep your investors in the loop on your progress. I used to write a simple quarterly e-mail to palmm's investors, structured along the following five themes: Funding, Team, Product, Market, and an Ask of them (e.g., help with connecting you to others). You can operationalize this leveraging e-mail marketing tools such as Constant Contact, but I didn't consider that necessary given the stage of our company.

## 3. Document Management

As a startup entrepreneur, you will generate a ton of documents that you may need to dig up again later. Think about all the NDAs, employee contracts, pitch deck versions, and more that you'll create. While it's a bit more time-consuming upfront, I am a big fan of organizing digital documents as best as possible—folder structure, file naming, trackers, and so on. All of this will help you stay organized. For more on that topic, take a peek at the *Keep Documents Organized* section on page 127.

A bunch of the documents that we discussed in previous chapters also need to be updated regularly. This includes pitch decks, various trackers, and financial projections (see the *online Scrappy Entrepreneur's toolkit*), Gantt charts, and cap tables. While the initial creation of these documents is a bigger effort, the revisions are a necessary maintenance job. Moreover, outsourcing to a less experienced individual is not an option as you need to know the backstory to grasp what needs to change.

When it comes to Gantt chart software and other collaboration tools, there are many online tools available that can help you. The ones I have tried are Asana, Trello, Wrike, and Monday, but there are plenty of others as well. Identifying the tool that suits you best is one task—consistently using it is another. In the early days at palmm, my cofounder and I were the only ones who had a view on the Gantt chart, which we had initially drawn on a whiteboard and then copied over into a spreadsheet. We weren't very good at sticking to it or at updating it as changes occurred. Once we had a few collaborators, we went through a stint of using our tool of choice (Wrike) more consistently. It did really help keep everyone on track and gave us a better sense of project status.

I mentioned cap tables earlier in this paragraph, as these also need regular updates. Our attorney handled that for us as our list of investors was relatively short. As things get more complex, there are software solutions that can help.

While a lot of these document management activities can be done in the moment, some require a bit more time. You can place a weekly hold on your calendar and then get it out of the way all in one go. Holly from Madorra (see page 12) likes doing this on Friday afternoons as she winds down from a busy week, when she is less likely to have e-mails landing in her inbox that need urgent attention. Start with an hour every week and see if you can get through it all within that time.

## 4. Light Manual Labor

When I brought up the topic of everything falling on your own plate as a scrappy entrepreneur, Bronwyn's (see the "From Another Perspective" insert on page 49) first reaction was: "I remember we had to print address labels and pack boxes for shipments ourselves!" Like Bronwyn, Justin and I spent hours preparing labels for our clinical study materials. Opening snail mail, cleaning up the office, and packing and transporting boxes when you're moving offices—all of this needs to get done by someone. If there aren't a lot of employees, that someone who does all this often ends up being the CEO or founder. Even if you are low on cash, if this really bothers you, you can leverage hourly workers (who you can find through TaskRabbit, Nextdoor, or a similar platform) or hire entry-level labor to reduce the burden. Bronwyn said that they were able to get help from a less experienced individual who was passionate about the company's mission and really wanted to get involved. This person started off helping with simple tasks. Over time, as she got exposed to more of the company's operations, she became a project manager. It was a win-win for everyone involved.

If you end up being the one who gets to do this, find ways to make it fun. I recall opening some drinks and chips together with my cofounder at the end of the day to make such tasks more of a team event than a chore. It's also what you make of it!

## 5. Vendor Selection

Another activity that can become time-consuming is vendor selection. The type of vendor I'm referring to isn't your next R&D partner, as those clearly contribute to the project's critical path. It's the search for the best bank, the most advantageous credit card, the most cost-effective insurance option, and the best software programs for various activities. For example, Justin and I spent a good amount of time researching cost versus features for document management software, comparing Dropbox to G Suite (now Google Workspace). At the time, Dropbox was a bit cheaper, but it didn't come with the collaboration features that G Suite offered. We were used to working with the more classical folder structure that Dropbox was built on and ended up selecting it for that reason. While the cost differences weren't huge, we felt switching vendors further down the line might be difficult, so we wanted to do the right thing from the beginning. I still think that that's the way to do it. What I wish we had done a better job of for such tasks, however, is taking a quick moment to jot down our selection criteria and the reasons for our decision. This would make it easier to reassess options as the company's needs shifted over time.

We didn't spend as much time comparing and contrasting banks. Silicon Valley Bank (SVB) and First Republic Bank (FRB) were the two most active players in our industry in the San Francisco Bay Area at the time. We had an FRB branch nearby. Choice made. It then came as a big surprise that both those banks failed a few years later. It is a scenario that hadn't even crossed our minds when we were listing pros and cons. What I take away from this turn of events is that it's worth revisiting certain choices over time. As you raise more money, it becomes more important to spread assets across multiple banks to mitigate the risk of losing access to all of your funds. Once again, simply jotting down the reasons for your decision will help you when you are ready to reassess.

Knowing what types of insurance you need for your startup, comparing insurance companies, and getting the policies to be right-sized are another topic for this chapter. Even writing about insurance raises my anxiety levels! At palmm, it started when we were negotiating our IP license agreement with Stanford University. Their standard template agreement stipulated that we were required to maintain general liability insurance, including product liability insurance. This general liability insurance needed to provide minimum limits of liability of $5 million according to the template. General liability insurance protects the company if others get injured or others' goods get damaged. Product liability insurance specifically protects against damage caused by product defects. As we didn't have product on the market yet, the product liability insurance requirement didn't make sense for us, so we got the license agreement amended accordingly. Also, the minimum limits of general liability of $5 million seemed high relative to what we owned and risked. As I was able to compare notes with other entrepreneurs, it became clear to me that other companies at similar stages had lower minimum limits in their policies (resulting in cheaper policies), so we ended up negotiating that down to $1 million.

In my research, I came across other types of insurance and started wondering if we needed those. This is where you can easily get lost. Beyond general liability insurance, which may include product liability insurance, common types of insurance that are relevant for pre-revenue startups include:

- Business property insurance, which covers your office and business property (e.g., laptops, office furniture) for theft, severe weather, fire, and more.
- Directors & Officers (D&O) insurance, which covers the startup's directors and officers in case of lawsuits involving such individuals related to theft of IP, copyright infringement, mismanaged funds, and more. This is something angel groups and other investors might ask for in particular.
- Employment Practices Liability Insurance (EPLI), which protects against lawsuits from employees. If you don't have employees beyond cofounders, this may be something you can skip.
- Worker's compensation insurance, which covers medical costs in case of workplace injury. Similar to EPLI, think about the utility of this type of insurance if your only employees are business owners.
- Errors & Omissions (E&O) insurance, which protects against lawsuits from clients when it comes to mistakes in professional services. If you don't have clients, it's probably not something you need—but you have to think broadly about who your clients might be. For example, in the health care industry, pre-revenue companies may still want this type of coverage if they are running clinical trials.
- Clinical Trials insurance, which pays for medical expenses if test subjects end up requiring medical treatment due to participation in the trial. It's obviously unnecessary if you don't run any clinical trials.
- Cyber liability insurance, which covers your business from cyber-attacks and accidental data leaks related to internal data and computer systems.

Nerdwallet and other websites offer reviews that can help you understand the scope of these types of insurances and sometimes help you compare options. There are also digital insurance companies that target startups with the goal of making things more straightforward and cost-effective. I find entrepreneur networks the most helpful for answers to questions on this topic, as it's easier to assume they are unbiased, and because the market and options continue to evolve.

As we're discussing insurance, one type of insurance you should definitely have on your radar is health care insurance for your employees, including yourself. Federal law does not require businesses with fewer than 50 employees to offer this benefit. palmm never reached this number, but, of course, Justin and I still needed health care insurance for ourselves. An alternative is to leverage parents' or spouse's insurance if possible, but this wasn't an option for either of us. So, we ended up using the state's health care exchange, Covered California. I am sure this system has evolved quite a bit since we used it, but we found it pretty straightforward at the time. Also, as we started thinking about hiring other employees, we wanted to make sure that our collaborators had access to health insurance. From a compensation perspective, you need to keep this in mind as you compete with companies that offer this perk. You can either have your employee leverage the health care exchange and compensate for this through salary or investigate the option of providing the benefit through the company. The latter may be more costly with no difference in the quality of the insurance.

Here is one final example of the type of vendor selection you'll have to do by yourself: booking travel. In contrast to big company employees, a scrappy entrepreneur doesn't have the luxury of a travel department, or dedicated software solutions, to assist with booking flights, hotels, and rental cars. When it's your own company, you have to do this the way you book your personal travel, and you're likely to be equally cost-conscious. Flight search engines such as Kayak, Expedia, and others are your friends, as are Airbnb and maybe even the couches of people you know across the country/world!

## 6. IP Portfolio Management

Securing the strongest possible IP position is a core business activity for any innovation-driven technology startup. As palmm's IP portfolio started expanding in volume and number of active geographies, I realized it became hard to keep track of what had been granted and what was still pending. My IP attorney created a nice summary for our data room. It contained a list of publicly available patents (with patent numbers, filing dates, and issuance dates where available), a list of filings we intended to move forward with, and what patent studies had been completed. I should have done a better job of keeping that summary up to date, as a year later I had to return to my law firm to ask them for a refresh.

The other aspect of managing an IP portfolio that gets tricky over time is knowing what payments need to be made and when. I'd like to help you understand what a typical timeline looks like and what costs you can expect. Figure 10.1 summarizes key milestones related to one patent lineage. The scenario assumes that you choose to first file a provisional patent application[9] with the USPTO, which is what scrappy entrepreneurs typically do as this approach delays bigger expenses. The scenario also assumes that you will ultimately file a utility patent to protect the way your invention works (as opposed to a design patent, which protects what your invention looks like) and that you will be filing a Patent Cooperation Treaty (PCT) patent application giving you the ability to gain protection in additional countries. Here is how to interpret Figure 10.1:

a. Filing a provisional patent application starts a clock of future activities and payments. By the 1-year mark, you'll need to have filed a PCT application and/or a U.S. nonprovisional patent application. If you don't file either of these, the provisional application will be considered to have been *abandoned* and no longer has value. It would be as though you had never submitted anything in the first place. The deadline to start seeking protection in other countries falls 30, 31, or 34 months (depending on the country) after the initial provisional filing, which is referred to as the *national-stage entry*.

b. Whenever an Office Action[11] comes in, the clock for that filing starts ticking again. As an example, for the first patent application related to palmm's technology, we received the first Office Action from the USPTO about 2.5 years after the initial provisional application filing. When you receive an Office Action from the USPTO, you typically have 3 months to respond, but you can extend that timeline by (typically) up to another 3 months for a relatively modest fee (U.S. Patent and Trademark Office 2024).

c. When a country's patent office lets you know that they agree with you that your application is a true invention, it is time to celebrate. But it's also time to plan ahead. After the so-called Notice of Allowance, you have just a limited time to submit a continuation or a divisional application (other types of patent applications that draw on content from previously filed ones), which takes considerable time and effort. If you don't, your patent family closes irreversibly.

The full timeline is dependent on the number of office responses and the time it takes for both parties (the patent office and you) to get back to each other. With the first patent filing, my cofounder Justin and I were eagerly waiting to get it granted, as that milestone added to our company's credibility for investors. For later patents, we were in no rush to make progress since costs racked up.

From the moment your patent has been granted, you need to start paying patent maintenance fees with the USPTO. There are third-party

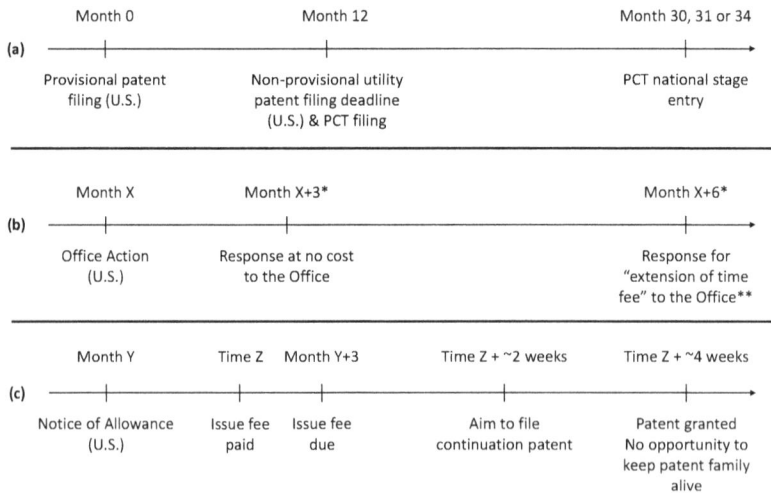

*Figure 10.1  Typical timeline for IP payments*

*\*The displayed timeline is typical, but some Office Actions have different response and extension times.*

*\*\*USPTO Patent extension of time fees can be found at www.uspto.gov/learning-and-resources/fees-and-payment/uspto-fee-schedule*

services that can alert you when these and other patent payments are due. The advantage of using such a service is that you don't have to keep track of timelines and requirements by country, but this obviously comes with an extra cost. Alternatively, you can add this type of information to your compliance calendar. Skip to page 123 for more on that suggestion.

IP mainly gets expensive because of attorney fees and various types of patent office fees. Additionally, you may have to pay inventors and licensors. You can find U.S. patent fees on the USPTO website (www. uspto.gov/learning-and-resources/fees-and-payment/uspto-fee-schedule). Startups with first-time entrepreneurs may be able to certify as a *micro entity* (or as a *small entity*), which comes with discounted fees.

# 7. Recurring Payments

Some of the activities that we covered in the previous sections, such as taxes, payroll, insurance, licenses, vendors, IP portfolio management, and software solution subscriptions, come with associated payments. There are a bunch of other things that require regular payments as well. To keep your work minimal, I recommend automating these payments as soon as they start. We got credit cards through Brex and then connected its software with our Quickbooks account to simplify the number of steps involved in the process. It wasn't fully seamless, but it was still better than having to do everything manually.

If you must prioritize your time when it comes to recurring pay- ments, it makes sense to focus on the biggest line items. For most innovation-driven technology startups, intellectual property will be on that list within the first few years. As missing IP-related deadlines can have value-destructing consequences for a company, budgeting for IP expenses is critical. Combined, the costs related to IP as described in the previous section (filing fees, Office Action fees, maintenance fees, attorney fees, in- ventor payments, licensing payments, and more) may become one of the biggest line items in your financial reports. While you can delay some of these costs, it is impossible to avoid them entirely. It is therefore a critical passive portion of a company's burn rate.

When it started to become clear in March 2020 that COVID-19 would reign the world for at least a few weeks, palmm was in a time of critical fundraising. I needed to understand how long the company could survive if we didn't raise our next round. A burn-rate tracker helped me gain clarity, and the biggest variable in it was IP. If we kept our full IP portfolio going, how long could we survive as a company? What if we prioritized just a few of the six countries in which we had applied? Did it make sense to continue to license the patent from Stanford University, or was that no longer mission-critical? This was a stressful scenario and, unfortunately, one that many companies may find themselves in at some point in their lifetime. While I hope you won't have to deal with it, if you do, the burn-rate tabs of the broader financial model in the Scrappy Entrepreneur's toolkit can help you strategize (see page 132 for details on how to access this toolkit).

## 8. Public Relations

PR professionals will balk at the idea of including public relations in a chapter about chores that *just have to get done*. Of course, I agree that developing your company's public image is important and that it can work with or against you when it comes to fundraising in particular. Still, during the pre-commercial stage when you are trying to prove that your idea is worthwhile, PR activities may feel like a distraction.

As an example, when you get started and have chosen a company name, you'll want to lock in the most appropriate web domain name for future online presence. I was lucky that my cofounder Justin knew what to do on that front, as he had done this in the past. We wanted *palmm.com*, but as that domain name was too expensive, we ended up with *palmm.co*. We decided not to create a proper website, as we were years away from going on the market. Later in our journey, we did create a second webpage to experiment with customer interactivity. This made me better appreciate the complexities that come with managing a website. As our secondary website included a simple survey to get input from potential future customers, we had to investigate the European Union's General Data Protection Regulation (GDPR) guidelines and ensure that the website's terms and conditions were adequate. I spent hours researching this, including reviewing the "terms and conditions" pages from similar sites.

As mentioned in the section on Follow-up Interactions on page 45, if your company website has a *news* section you will want to update this page on a regular basis. If you don't, it may give potential investors the impression that things aren't going well. A similar story holds for social media presence. Creating a business LinkedIn page may be straightforward enough, but keeping it active gets trickier over time. If you need help staying on top of it, this could potentially be a fun activity for an intern.

## 9. Summing It Up

When I read through this chapter after writing it, my first reaction was: I hope I won't be deterring anyone from starting a business! But my second emotion was one of pride. As a scrappy entrepreneur you have to deal with so much that successfully navigating the maze becomes an accomplishment that others will envy. Despite so much to stay on top of, it is all worth it.

With that said, I hope you feel more prepared about what to expect with this chapter in your back pocket.

# CHAPTER 11

# How to Go About It

The previous chapter already included some tips to help you manage the various chores that will come your way as a scrappy entrepreneur. In this chapter, we'll focus on my favorite 12 to help you stay on top of it all. I had to painstakingly learn about these either in the moment or after the fact. Adopt what feels right for you from the very beginning!

## 1. Create a Compliance Calendar

Creating a compliance calendar is a tip I got from Holly from Madorra (see page 12), so I can't really take credit for it. While a compliance calendar is a real thing that you can read about on the web, here is how I recommend going about it:

1. Create a separate calendar in the software that you typically use, whether it is Google Calendar, iCal, Outlook, or something else.
2. Add deadlines for action items related to the types of topics that we covered in the previous chapter. For example, if annual reports for the state of Delaware are due March 1st, add an annually recurring calendar entry for that topic on that day.
3. Then add at least two reminders for each deadline—one reminder 3 months ahead of the actual deadline and another one a month ahead of the deadline. For the annual reports for the state of Delaware, this means adding a first reminder on December 1st and a second one on February 1st. You can adjust this schedule to make it work best for you.

As the number of required activities adds up, you'll have peace of mind knowing that you will be reminded of upcoming deliverables in plenty of time and won't have to clock late nights trying to meet deadlines you didn't see coming.

Having all this info centralized in one place may even help you determine whether you need to start outsourcing anything and simplify an eventual transition.

## 2. Block Time to Get It Done

Find a fixed time in your week during which you get this stuff done. For example, block an hour each Friday. And if you are following the previous tip, you'll know exactly what to focus on during that time. This practice can help in small and large companies alike, as I've experienced firsthand. Whether you use the time to deal with the activities from the previous chapter or to get mandatory trainings out of the way, if you don't proactively block time, you will always find yourself having to squeeze these tasks in at suboptimal moments.

Dedicating time to this type of activity will minimize procrastination and help you understand how much effort you need to put in so that you can gauge if it's still within an acceptable range. It will also allow you to stay focused during the rest of your week, as you'll know that you'll be able to get to these tasks. If the time you picked doesn't work one week, you can shift the block by a few hours or move it to a different day.

## 3. Leverage Software Solutions

Don't forget that your time is money, too. Some of the software or services you already have access to may have built-in functionalities that can make you more efficient without incurring any additional costs.

For example, to deal with the recurring payments from the *Recurring Payments* section on page 119, set up automated payments in your banking or credit card system so that you can set and forget. If this sounds obvious to you, that's great!

As another example, your e-mail client software (Gmail, Apple Mail, Microsoft Outlook, or whichever one you use) may enable you to send e-mails at a scheduled time, rather than the moment you hit *Send*. Thanks to such a feature, you can decouple your work time from the time your recipient receives the message. Figuring out the best time to send e-mails is a science, as you'll learn if you Google the topic. All in all, mornings are often optimal to ensure that your message doesn't get buried by other e-mails the recipient receives throughout the day. It's a trick that I have used many a time to maximize my chances of receiving a response from potential investors and other important stakeholders. It also means that you can prepare e-mails all at once without sending them out in one go, so that you can optimize your own response time. As the natural language processing capabilities of artificial intelligence (AI) continue to advance, text generation for investor e-mails may become a breeze. That said, personalizing these e-mails will be even more important to truly catch the recipient's attention.

Beyond the products you or your company already own, you can invest in other software solutions to lessen your burden on various fronts. Think about accounting software, expense management software, payroll support, and even password and contract/electronic signature management software as per the examples in previous chapters. These can be cost-effective if you make the right choices.

Try these types of software before you buy them if you can, or at least don't commit to a full year if you can test them out for a month.

## 4. Get Cost-Effective Help for Simple Tasks

Once you have a minimal amount of cash available, take advantage of opportunities to benefit from cheap help. This can range from hourly workers (e.g., through TaskRabbit or Amazon Mechanical Turk), to interns, to experts who are not in it for the money—or at least not for upfront cash. As Bronwyn (from Tueo Health) expressed it (see page 113): Look for win-win situations. Someone who is looking to get involved but does not have the right background may be more than happy to get started with a few mundane tasks while learning more about an endeavor that is meaningful to them. We took that approach when I realized that I was spending way too much time ordering R&D supplies, and in Quickbooks, Brex, Gusto, and so on. There happened to be an intern doing this type of work for a different company at our incubator, and she had some hours to spare. We were able to leverage her help. In a similar vein, I have heard from entrepreneurs who have been happy with support from a part-time, remote executive assistant.

Maria from Medina Medical (see page 50) went all in on this approach. She was lucky enough to find someone who could spend a couple of hours a week on writing and document management who had a lot of experience, was in a financially favorable spot, and—above all—was someone Maria felt she could fully trust. Maria's key piece of advice? Figure out what you're not good at and find a way to delegate that so that you can focus on what you do well! I'll add that you should keep Figure 5.1 in mind so that you bring in someone with the appropriate level of expertise.

## 5. Log Step-by-Step Instructions

Have you ever been frustrated that you had to find an answer to a question again, even if you knew you'd already done this in the past? I often have that with Excel formulas: I'll spend 20 minutes figuring out how to get what I need, and then a few months later I need the exact same thing and I no longer remember how it's done. The solution is simple: Just jot down a brief version of the steps you used to get there in a digital notebook, and you'll save yourself time in the future.

You can use this approach when you apply for a new grant and have to navigate multiple websites in the process, or when you submit your company profile to be considered by an angel group. The information will definitely come in handy if you have to reapply.

When you create a new password, make sure you save it, either using a password management software (I use LastPass, just as an example) or by writing it down as part of the process. This is a tip that comes from my personal experiences trying to do and redo registrations that were required for an SBIR grant application. There were multiple signature steps as part of the process, and I hadn't kept notes about what password I had used where. I spent hours problem-solving on my own, and then on the phone with the service center, to fix the issue.

## 6. Create and Maintain Trackers

The extent to which you'll want to adopt this sixth tip will depend on your personality type. People who are planners tend to be keener on creating and managing trackers than more spontaneous folks. Still, I highly recommend making trackers for activities that get complex over time—fundraising in particular. See section *Keeping Track of It All*, on page 47, for more on this. Such a tracker ultimately fulfills the role of a Customer Relationship Management (CRM) tool. The tracker not only helps you stay on top of who is still in the potential investor mix and when you should follow up but also helps you remember where you are in the conversation. Personally, when I'm talking with someone, my naïve tendency is to think that I won't forget what was said. But over time, having so many similar conversations with different investors, I invariably lost track of the details if I didn't keep some records of the key discussion points. As Large Language Models (LLMs) keep improving, those will help you find your way through these notes even better.

For those who aren't averse to maintaining trackers, you can use the same technique to keep lists of potential candidates for a vacancy, for logging NDAs and any nuances within, for keeping an overview of your IP lineages, and more. These can be simple lists in Excel/Google Sheets/Numbers with some carefully chosen columns, such as the templates included in the online Scrappy Entrepreneur's toolkit (see page 132 for details on how to access this toolkit).

## 7. Log Decision Criteria for Key Choices

Once you have made a key decision, take a moment to pen down the pros and cons of that choice in your digital notebook, so that you can more easily reassess when needed. The decision can relate to anything from vendor selection (as discussed on page 113), to R&D. If you want to make sure you reassess at some point, you can leverage your compliance calendar (see page 123) to help remind you.

## 8. Keep Documents Organized

To make sure you can easily retrieve documents in the future, follow this guidance:

a. Give each file a structured name. I start each file with a date (YYYYMMDD), followed by a description of the content, followed by a version number, with each of these sections divided by underscore symbols. Even for the purpose of writing this book, I was able to quickly retrieve early and late versions of palmm's pitch deck team slides thanks to this structure (see Figures 7.1 and 7.2).

b. Structure folders logically. This may be old-fashioned, as the future may drive us away from folders altogether. But as long as unstructured search isn't fully optimal, a logical folder structure will certainly not do any harm. The data room folder structure shown in Figure 2.3 is an example of this.

c. Use a digital notebook. Being able to search notes can be a lifesaver. The searchable aspect of these digital notebooks (Evernote, OneNote, Google Keep, and others) has come in handy for me on many an occasion when I remembered just a word but wanted to find more.

## 9. Stop Subscriptions You No Longer Need

This tip is about helping you be frugal. Monthly subscriptions are great in the sense that you don't need to have a ton of cash available upfront to be able to get access to a service, but they are easily forgotten. During a time at palmm when we had contractors come and go, I kept an eye on the number of seats for various software subscriptions. If there is something you no longer need, take a minute to downsize or cancel subscriptions. It's as simple as that!

## 10. Right-size It and Keep Calm!

When you're starting out, every dollar counts. But if you can't fit everything in your day anymore, you have to focus on what is more important. When the COVID-19 pandemic hit, my flight to a pitch event got canceled. Initially I fought to get my money back, but ultimately realized the fight wasn't worth it. It had been a cheap ticket, and I had more important things to focus on than spending hours on the phone with American Airlines customer service. And I realized I could always make time for it later.

Gabriel from Enspectra Health (see page 46) helped put this in perspective for me: "Don't sweat every little thing! An occasional late fee does not mean the end of your company."

# 11. Ask Fellow Entrepreneurs

If there is anything I learned in the process of getting guest contributions to this book, it's that my fellow entrepreneurs have a lot of expertise that could have benefited me in the moment. Of course, we're always pressed for time, but in hindsight I should have asked more *random* questions to entrepreneurs that I met at various events to learn from them. The topics we discussed in this section of the book are things that any other entrepreneur can help you with, even if they work in a different industry.

If you use your network to its fullest extent, it will make your bonds even stronger as you realize how you can help each other and feel less isolated. So, whenever you go to a networking event, make it a goal to return with at least one new insight from a fellow entrepreneur. How about using this book as a conversation starter?

I must acknowledge that it takes a bit of courage to have such conversations. In the moment, it may feel like you're trying to measure yourself up against other entrepreneurs—even if you know that that's not helpful or needed. Try to let go of that competitive feeling. I found the monthly CEO-only meeting at Fogarty Innovation helpful for this.

# 12. Revise Your Approach When Needed

Keep an eye on the amount of time you are devoting to all of this. If it is more than a handful of hours a week, simplify where you can and look for outsourcing solutions. I like time management techniques such as the Eisenhower *urgency/importance* framework to help with prioritization, based on *The 7 Habits of Highly Effective People* (Covey 2004). Prioritize tasks that are urgent and important. If something is urgent but not important, consider delegating the task. If something is important but not urgent, set aside some time in the (near) future to get to it. And, critically, do not waste your time on things that are neither urgent nor important. If you decide to outsource, remind yourself of the tips in "Leverage software solutions" (see page 124) and "Get cost-effective help for simple tasks" (see page 125) earlier in this chapter.

# CHAPTER 12

# Key Takeaways from Part 3—All the Small Stuff That Adds Up

## 💡 Key Learnings

1. Expect to have to deal with a lot of random things.
2. Create a compliance calendar.
3. Block time to get this stuff done.
4. Leverage software solutions.
5. Get cheap help for simple tasks, looking for win-win situations.
6. Write down steps for things you don't do often.
7. Create and regularly update trackers.
8. Jot down reasons for key choices so that you can more easily reassess them.
9. Keep documents organized.
10. Right-size it and keep calm.
11. Stop subscriptions you no longer need.
12. Ask fellow entrepreneurs for helpful tips and tricks.
13. Keep an eye on the amount of time you are devoting to all of this. If it's more than a handful of hours per week, look for outsourcing solutions.

## Key Tools and Resources Provided

- References to many vendors who can help you stay on top of all the small stuff that adds up can be found throughout this book section.
- Incorporation package generator from Cooley GO Docs: www.CooleyGo.com

- Website of the Delaware Division of Corporations, where Delaware corporations file their annual report and pay business entity tax: https://corp.delaware.gov
- Website of the California Franchise Tax Board, with information on doing business in California: www.ftb.ca.gov/file/business
- Website of the California Secretary of State, where companies operating out of California need to file an annual or biennial Statement of Information: https://bizfileonline.sos.ca.gov
- Website of the state of California's Employment Development Department (EDD), which employers with employees in California need to register on: https://eddservices.edd.ca.gov
- Website of the USPTO website, with helpful information on filing patents in the United States and associated fees: www.uspto.gov/learning-and-resources/fees-and-payment/uspto-fee-schedule
- Financial model template including burn-rate calculations: Included in the Scrappy Entrepreneur's toolkit
  (In the document, see tabs following the "Costs=>" tab)

Note: Visit veroniquepeiffer.com to receive a copy of the Scrappy Entrepreneur's toolkit.

# In Closing

With the insights from this book under your belt, I hope that you feel more prepared to start fundraising, confident that you'll be able to avoid common mistakes as you build your team, and equipped to efficiently handle the various unavoidable tasks that come with being a scrappy entrepreneur. Because—let's be clear—you will not only be a (co)founder and potentially a chief officer of your company, but you'll also act as the executive assistant, accountant, controller, head of HR, and more.

Reading about palmm Co. throughout this book may have you wondering: How is palmm doing? What's next? It's a question I hear all the time.

When the first COVID-19 cases appeared in the United States (in the very same hospital where our company was located, by the way), we were low on cash. The burn-rate tracker I created (see the *Recurring Payments* section on page 119) indicated that we could survive till July 2020 if we did not make any changes to our spending levels. It was early Q2 2020, and I had to make a guess on whether the pandemic would be behind us in a month or two or it would last until the end of 2020 and beyond. As my instinct told me it would be the latter, I could think of two options: (1) keeping palmm going without making changes, knowing that—if I couldn't raise additional funding—it would be over and done within a few months, and (2) hibernating before we hit zero dollars on our bank account. The latter would enable us to keep our IP going, thereby maintaining our most valuable assets and keeping alive the possibility of reviving the company in a better economic environment. The staff at Fogarty Innovation helped me work through these considerations. I also brought our investors along on the journey by gauging their interest in participating in a bridge round. I went for the hibernation option. I gave all of our contributors a heads-up soon after making the decision so that they could begin making other plans. And I started looking for a stable job myself, which I found at Genentech, Inc. I closed operations of palmm in California by filing the final state tax return but kept the Delaware C-Corp open by continuing to file the annual reports with the accompanying payments. To come back to the topic of only bringing on angel investors who are familiar with the risks of angel investing (see page 19), I am glad I listened to that advice. My investor base was very understanding of the situation once the decision was made.

During nights and weekends, I maintain our IP portfolio and keep our accounting up to date. As of early 2025, we have not resumed operations. When the timing may be right to do so is fluid: It just depends on when someone (usually a founder) decides that the conditions are favorable enough to get back to it and put in the time to fundraise and/or advance the technology. In my eyes, the equation has not sufficiently changed since the beginning of the pandemic. So, there has been no big financial return for us; nor have we been able to help patients with the technology that we invented. It pains me to say that, yet it is the hard reality. I am certainly not the only entrepreneur who ended up in such a scenario.

When I moved to the San Francisco Bay Area, I heard many times that failures should be celebrated. Among Stanford Biodesign Innovation Fellows and alumni, we often talked about holding a panel with CEOs of *failed* companies to share their learnings. We never got around to doing this. It's always the wins that get the attention, and at best the entrepreneur will laugh away the struggles and poor decisions they made along the way. Just to be clear, I am all for celebrating successes. It is so hard to achieve it that, when there is a happy end, we should make the time to properly acknowledge it and learn from it. But we should also realize that there are learnings from a company that does not end in a big financial or commercial win that are equally interesting and inspiring. I hope that has become clear to you from reading this book.

Also, pretty much anyone who has done it will agree with me that the line between a successful or failed venture is wafer-thin. As I've mentioned before, I am a fan of the "How I Built This" podcast, in which former NPR journalist Guy Raz interviews one successful entrepreneur per episode. Prompted by the question—"How much of your success was down to luck versus hard work/skill?"—virtually everyone acknowledges that at least a bit of luck is needed to be successful. And a success in the eyes of one person can look like a failure to another. Many consider a so-called exit, the acquisition of the startup or an Initial Public Offering (IPO), at a desired multiple (e.g., 5 times, 10 times) as a win. Others focus on commercial success. Unfortunately, I know too many companies that reached one of these, but not the other. A pre-commercial technology gets acquired, but then the buyer's focus shifts and the technology is never commercialized. Or a medtech startup gets their product to market and saves or improves the lives of many patients but cannot find a way to make an exit.

Even though palmm did not reach a successful exit, what a ride has it been! Never a dull moment. If you compare it to taking care of a baby, the difference is that the outcome is even less predictable. When your child is throwing a tantrum or when you just don't know what is best for them, at least you can have some peace of mind knowing that, most of the time, it will be all right in the end. With a startup, most end up failing.

And still, it has been worth it. It takes many to try for one to be successful. Those who contributed to the palmm journey will agree that this experience helped them grow professionally. I definitely did! When the accountability for so many functions falls on you, you learn more. As I'm currently working for a *big company*, I see it around me all the time: I have a much better understanding of what's happening in other departments because they were just a fraction of my entire job at palmm. The entrepreneurs I interviewed for this book who have moved on from their startups acknowledge the same.

What remains is for me to wish you good luck as a scrappy entrepreneur. Strap in, enjoy every minute of it, and make it happen!

# Notes

1.  Fogarty Innovation is a nonprofit, educational medtech incubator with a staff of industry veterans that provide intensive coaching to entrepreneurs and startup teams. However, the organization no longer offers cash equity positions to its incubated companies.

2.  If you are not familiar with *convertible debt, Simple agreement for future equity (Safe* (Levy, n.d.)*)*, and *priced rounds*, and the differences among those, I recommend browsing www.CooleyGO.com, a website with helpful resources created by law firm Cooley LLP.

3.  For more on the important distinctions between ownership equity or notes that can convert to ownership equity, I recommend browsing the CooleyGO website (www.CooleyGO.com).

4.  A cap table or capitalization table is a document that lists the company's owners and ownership stake.

5.  Dead equity is equity that is owned by individuals who are no longer active in the company. It is typically considered undesirable as it leaves less stock to incentivize future contributors.

6.  The Berkus method is a simple method to value startups. The highest possible valuation using this method is $2.5 million (Berkus, 2016).

7.  *Vesting* is a legal term indicating that receiving a benefit fully is subject to the amount of time the beneficiary remains in position. For example, if the beneficiary receives 1,200 stock options for a year-long contract with a monthly vesting schedule, they would have the right to 100 stock options for every month of that year. If they leave the company early after 5 months, they would receive a total of 500 stock options.

8.  For more on vesting, see note 7 above. A cliff, as part of a vesting schedule, is an amount of time that has to pass before a beneficiary can receive any portion of the benefit. For example, if the beneficiary receives 1,200 stock options for a year-long contract with a monthly vesting schedule and a 6-month cliff, they would have the right to 100 stock options for every month of that year. If they leave the company early after 5 months (i.e., prior to the 6-month cliff), they would not receive any stock options.

9.  A provisional application for patent can be filed without a formal patent claim, oath or declaration, or any prior art statement. It provides the means to establish an early effective filing date in a later filed nonprovisional patent application (U.S. Patent and Trademark Office, n.d.) and provides a lower-cost first patent filing in the United States.

10. Keep in mind that company logos are copyrighted material. While a lot of startups put logos from other companies on their slides, you typically need to get permission for this from those companies.

11. An Office Action is an official letter from a patent office. For example, an Office Action may indicate that the patent examiner has decided to reject the patent application and detail the reasons for the rejection.

# About the Author

Véronique Peiffer, PhD is an entrepreneur and life sciences professional. Formerly a management consultant at McKinsey & Company, she cofounded and led palmm Co., a company focused on the development of therapeutic bioelectronics. This pivotal experience served as the primary inspiration for The Scrappy Entrepreneur. Véronique holds a leadership role at Genentech, Inc. and teaches the next generation of health technology entrepreneurs as an associate director of the Stanford Mussallem Center for Biodesign. She lives in the San Francisco Bay Area with her husband and two children.

# Acknowledgments

With two-thirds of this book devoted to the excitement and challenges that come with finding investors and team members for a startup, it's only natural that these actors deserve special acknowledgment in my story.

Thank you to those who organize pitch competitions or make grants and other resources available to young startups. Your efforts are invaluable in making novel ideas become a reality. A special thanks to the Stanford Mussallem Center for Biodesign, Cardinal Ventures, BASES (Business Association of Stanford Entrepreneurial Students), Spectrum (Stanford Center for Clinical and Translational Research and Education), the Wallace H. Coulter Foundation, the James Gallagher Patell Fund, StartX, VentureWell E-Team, the UCSF-Stanford Pediatric Device Consortium, Fogarty Innovation, and Medtech Innovator for providing this type of support to (the project preceding) palmm Co.

Many thanks also to all early-stage investors out there for being willing to take financial risk and thereby spur innovation. To those individuals who stepped up to invest in palmm, thank you for your trust and support along the way.

palmm Co. wouldn't have existed if my cofounder, Justin Huelman, had not shared with me the medical need that he had observed. Justin, I am truly grateful that you trusted me to embark on this entrepreneurial journey together and that you continued to see a friend on the other side even when things were a bit chaotic.

I'm equally thankful for those who chose to work with us as team members or close collaborators. Some of you spent a significant amount of time with us: Jarren Baldwin, Kei Castleberry, Daniel Francis, Thi-Vu Huynh, Chris Pell, Professor Dr. Marlyanne Pol-Rodriguez, Fiona Sander, and Peter Townshend. Your expertise and efforts made an important difference for palmm.

I am so grateful for the many other thought partners and role models who have shaped my entrepreneurial path over the past decade. If readers of this book stumbled on any wisdom, chances are that I got the insight through a conversation with one of those supporters. When I moved to the United States to participate in Stanford University's Biodesign Innovation Fellowship, I had no idea that I would be immediately immersed in such a vibrant network of innovators. I continue to learn from the community of faculty, mentors, and alumni that Professor Emeritus Dr. Paul Yock laid the foundations for, and that Dr. Josh Makower is now leading. I was doubly lucky when palmm got to join Fogarty Innovation (founded by physician inventor Dr. Thomas Fogarty), just when Andrew Cleeland took the reins there. The mentorship I received from the incubator staff—Greg Bakan, Denise Zarins, Corinne Landphere, Mike Regan, and others—went above and beyond. I also couldn't be more grateful for my peers at fellow companies-in-residence to be willing to share their learnings and rolodexes with me. Case in point: Seven entrepreneurs from these communities provided their insights specifically for this book. Maria Aboytes, Eric Chehab, Bronwyn Harris, Anand Parikh, Holly Rockweiler, Gabriel Sanchez, and Iris Wedeking—thank you for contributing.

Beyond these two networks, I have crossed paths with so many people who are willing to take the time to mentor the newer generation of entrepreneurs. In terms of role models, I'll proudly include my dad for his persistence and willingness to reinvent his business as markets shifted.

Writing a book is an endeavor in and of itself. I was delighted when I heard back from Business Expert Press that they saw the value in this work, and I am grateful for their mission to fill a gap for business students and professionals. Two people (beyond my family) believed in me and encouraged me to keep going: my leadership coach, Corinne Landphere, and my good friend, Amalia De Luca. A heartfelt thanks to the two of you for always cheering me on!

The version in the hands of the readers now is so much better than the initial manuscript thanks to careful proofreading by several individuals. My mom, an English major, was the first to help ensure my grammar was on point. Greg Bakan provided insightful perspectives from his experience with multiple startups and a startup incubator. True to his style, he knew how to sharpen my learnings on entrepreneurship even during this process. As a freshly minted graduate of the Stanford Biodesign Innovation Fellowship, Marie Uncovska, PhD, applied the lens of an entrepreneur in the earliest stages. Amy Embert with Resonance IP Law was kind enough to review a draft of certain sections related to intellectual property. And Stacey Paris McCutcheon gave the draft manuscript a full makeover. Readers can thank her for her attention to detail, which helped drastically improve the flow of this book. Finally, I would never want to publish anything without my husband Moïse's stamp of approval, as his input is always thoughtful and well-rounded.

And to my two sweetest little ones: You made it delightfully harder for me to write this book! Everything you do fills me with amazement and joy. Thank you for giving me a much more balanced perspective on life.

# References

Angel Capital Association. 2024. "FAQs for Angels & Entrepreneurs." Accessed July 28, 2024. https://angelcapitalassociation.org/faqs/.

Berkus, Dave. 2016. "After 20 Years: Updating the Berkus Method of Valuation." November 4. Accessed July 21, 2024. https://berkonomics.com/?p=2752.

Blank, Steve, and Bob Dorf. 2020. *The Startup Owner's Manual: The Step-By-Step Guide for Building a Great Company.* Wiley.

Bureau of Labor Statistics. n.d. "Occupational Employment and Wage Statistics." Accessed July 13, 2024. www.bls.gov/oes/.

Chron Contributor. 2020. "Differences Between Cost Method & Equity Method." September 20. Accessed July 13, 2024. https://smallbusiness.chron .com/differences-between-cost-method-equity-method-65668.html.

Conley, Chip. 2007. *Peak: How Great Companies Get Their Mojo from Maslow.* Jossey-Bass.

Covey, Stephen. 2004. *The 7 Habits of Highly Effective People: Powerful Lessons in Personal Change.* Free Press.

Delaware Division of Corporations. 2019. "Corporate Annual Report Information and Franchise Tax Fees." September 1. Accessed August 2, 2024. https://corp.delaware.gov/paytaxes/.

Doolittle, James, Patricia Walker, Thomas Mills, and Jane Thurston. 2016. "Hyperhidrosis: An Update on Prevalence and Severity in the United States." *Archives Dermatological Research* 308 (10): 743–749.

Horowitz, Ben. 2014. *The Hard Thing About Hard Things: Building a Business When There Are No Easy Answers.* Harper Business.

Hvidkjaer, Kim. 2022. *How to F*ck Up Your Startup: The Science Behind Why 90% of Companies Fail—and How You Can Avoid It.* Matt Holt.

Johnson, Stefanie K., David R. Hekman, and Elsa T. Chan. 2016. "If There's Only One Woman in Your Candidate Pool, There's Statistically No Chance She'll Be Hired." April 26. Accessed July 30, 2024. https://hbr.org/2016/04 /if-theres-only-one-woman-in-your-candidate-pool-theres-statistically-no -chance-shell-be-hired.

Lencioni, Patrick. 2002. *The Five Dysfunctions of a Team: A Leadership Fable.* Jossey-Bass.

Levy, Carolynn. n.d. "Safe Financial Documents." Accessed July 20, 2024. www .ycombinator.com/documents.

Mendelson, Jason, and Brad Feld. 2019. *Venture Deals: The Science Behind Why 90% of Companies Fail—and How You Can Avoid It.* Wiley.

Nth round. n.d. "Psst…You Don't Need to be an Accredited Investor." Accessed July 12, 2024. www.nthround.com/blog/psst-you-dont-need-to-be -an-accredited-investor.

Reed, Chris J. 2015. "LinkedIn's New Inmail Policy: How to Enable It for You." January 15. Accessed October 15, 2024. www.linkedin.com/pulse /linkedins-new-inmail-policy-how-enable-you-chris-j-reed/.

Riemer, David. 2021. *Get Your Startup Story Straight: The Definitive Storytelling Framework for Innovators and Entrepreneurs.* River Grove Books.

Ries, Eric. 2011. *The Lean Startup: How Today's Entrepreneurs Use Continuous Innovation to Create Radically Successful Businesses.* Crown Business.

Rutherford, Matthew W. 2015. *Strategic Bootstrapping.* Business Expert Press.

Sarna, Surbhi. 2023. *Without a Doubt: How to Grow from Underrated to Unbeatable.* Simon & Schuster.

Startup Genome LLC. *Global Startup Ecosystem Report.* San Francisco, CA: Startup Genome, 2019. https://startupgenome.com/reports/global-startup -ecosystem-report-2019.

U.S. Patent and Trademark Office. n.d. "Provisional Application for Patent." Accessed August 2, 2024. www.uspto.gov/patents/basics/apply/provisional -application.

U.S. Patent and Trademark Office. 2024. "USPTO Fee Schedule." July 1. Accessed August 1, 2024. www.uspto.gov/learning-and-resources/fees-and-payment /uspto-fee-schedule.

U.S. Securities and Exchange Commission. 2024. "Accredited Investors." June 27. www.sec.gov/education/capitalraising/building-blocks/accredited-investor.

Virk, Rizwan. 2020. *Startup Myths and Models: What You Won't Learn in Business School.* Columbia University Press.

Voss, Christopher, and Tahl Raz. 2016. *Never Split the Difference: Negotiating as If Your Life Depended on It.* Harper Business.

Zenios, Stefanos, Josh Makower, Paul Yock, Todd J. Brinton, Uday N. Kumar, Lyn Denend, and Thomas M. Krummel. 2009. *Biodesign: The Process of InnovatingMedical Technologies.* Cambridge University Press.

# Index

www.ingramcontent.com/pod-product-compliance
Lightning Source LLC
Chambersburg PA
CBHW061317220326
41599CB00026B/4918